Praise for Raising A+ Human Beings

"However hard it may be to carve out the hours to read an inspiring piece of work with the detail and attention it deserves, I'm honored to have had the opportunity to study this amazing work! . . . This guide to how A+ schools shape A+ human beings conveys the magic of Bruce Powell and Ron Wolfson's exceptional careers in educational leadership in powerful, practical language. Drawing on a wealth of wisdom, knowledge, and experience—from students and educators, from the Talmud, from popular culture, from their own children as well as grandchildren—we learn the tools to successfully deliver the 'sacred task' of education. A must-read for current and future school leaders."

—PAUL BERNSTEIN, CEO, Prizmah: Center for Jewish Day Schools

"The title of this terrific book, *Raising A+ Human Beings*, claims that a school's true excellence is measured not by its students' test scores and college acceptances but by their individual and communal acts of kindness and responsibility. Leaders shape such excellence through an explicit curriculum of words, stories, and rituals. The entire school community consistently voices and enacts this curriculum in the everyday experiences of classroom, hallway, cafeteria, and playing field. The authors offer practical guidance on how to create inspiring school culture. They enliven their advice by illustrating each element of the who, what, and how of this work through vignettes—all engaging, a few even hilarious—drawn from their real lives as A+ educators."

—CHERYL FINKEL, board chair, The Covenant Foundation;
former head of school, The Epstein School, Atlanta, Georgia

"I have become a real believer in conscious leadership, and this book helps our school leaders consciously decide the culture they want to create in their schools and work, partnering with the students, teachers, administration, and families to make it happen. This book illustrates how that intentionality can create a school we would all be proud to be a part of. It is not only a blueprint, it is an inspiration."

—JANE TAUBENFELD COHEN, Jewish Day School leadership coach

"It doesn't take long to realize that *Raising A+ Human Beings* is more than just a book about the experiences and contributions of two great Jewish educators. Steeped in Jewish wisdom and tradition, this book is a reimagination of the possibility of Jewish education. Both descriptive and prescriptive, *Raising A+ Human Beings* provides a profound, and at times radical, framework for Jewish education that is both desirable and necessary in the world today."

—DAVID BRYFMAN, proud CEO, The Jewish Education Project, New York City

"We've learned so much about what makes a school and its students successful in life as well as in learning—and 'culture' is a vital and important part of it. Experienced, thoughtful, and creative educators Bruce Powell and Ron Wolfson have played a critical role in helping us understand this through their direct experience in fostering the values of A+ cultures in day and synagogue schools. Now they have distilled the essence of the lessons learned for us so that all of our Jewish schools can see how to do it and how our children can benefit from their knowledge. An essential read for all those who work with and care about our young people—from heads of schools and their boards to educators and camp staff."

—HARLENE WINNICK APPELMAN, executive director,
The Covenant Foundation, New York City

"The field of Jewish day school education, as well as Jewish education in general, is fortunate to be the recipient of a new volume focused on the critical topic of building school culture in a Jewish setting. A volume that has had a powerful impact on me is *Shaping School Culture* by Terrence Deal and Kent Peterson. What Bruce Powell and his coauthor, Ron Wolfson, have effectively done is to create a richly Jewish version of how to shape school culture. They have included case studies, Jewish values, traditional texts, and an expansive lens through which to learn about the challenges of Jewish culture building. Among the most useful parts of the book are the workbook-style questions that guide the reader on a successful journey toward Jewish culture building at its best. Bravo to Powell and Wolfson on this stellar accomplishment!"

—RABBI DR. JOSH ELKIN, former national director of PEJE,
Partnership for Excellence in Jewish Education

"Dr. Bruce Powell, with an assist by Dr. Ron Wolfson, has taken his years of leadership, expertise, and experience and crafted a volume teeming with insight for the Jewish community. This book reads like a conversation between the reader and two veteran educators, asking probing questions and offering applicable wisdom. You will think about organizational culture in a more nuanced and deliberative way after reading it. The ideas and examples throughout the book illustrate what Dr. Powell created and how you can improve your own practices. What a gift to the field of Jewish education!"

—DR. RACHEL LERNER, dean, Graduate Center for Jewish Education,
American Jewish University, Los Angeles, California

"Bruce Powell, a leader in day school education for more than forty years, shares, in very clear and practical terms, his firsthand experience in the 'Who,' 'What,' and 'How' of creating a school culture that nurtures A+ human beings. The insights of Ron Wolfson, who has, over decades, focused on the importance of relationship building in every setting of Jewish engagement, add to an already compelling narrative, filled with real-life anecdotes. The lessons of this instructive and uplifting book can contribute to the success of any organization. An A+ read!"

—**DR. GIL GRAFF**, executive director, Builders of Jewish Education, Los Angeles, California

"The best school culture is created intentionally, and so much of a school's impact in the community is rooted in the culture we create. Dr. Powell, with his vast experience in Jewish day schools, explicitly names the aspects of culture to which a school leader must be attuned. By sharing his experiences at de Toledo High School, Dr. Powell— along with commentaries from Dr. Ron Wolfson—helps illustrate how people, values, and process bring this culture to life. This easy-to-digest book, full of wisdom and humor, is a must-read for all school leaders."

—**DR. ERICA ROTHBLUM**, head of school, Pressman Academy of Temple Beth Am, Los Angeles, California

"While for others, this book is an incredibly useful collection of anecdotes, values, and practical approaches, I was one of the lucky educators who worked for and with Dr. Powell in building de Toledo High School. Through our sixteen years together, I witnessed the magic of creating a school that 'talked the talk' and 'walked the walk' on instilling a culture of A+ human beings. This book is a fantastic guide to the values and culture necessary to create and grow a successful values-based school."

—**MARK SHPALL**, head of school, de Toledo High School, Woodland Hills, California

"This book is an incredible reminder of the power of a Jewish day school that understands the power of connections and relationships. It all trickles down from the top. In order to raise A+ students, we—the administration, board, staff, and educators, as well as parents, grandparents, and caregivers—*must* model A+ behavior in order to raise generations of *mensches*!"

—HAVI HALL, LCSW, board member,
Gideon Hausner Jewish Day School, Palo Alto, California

"When you open this book, you sit at the feet of master educators as they explain: (1) the vital importance of creating a culture that fosters values integral to an exemplary Jewish day school (or other Jewish institution), (2) key attributes of that culture, and (3) how it is created and by whom. The myriad heartwarming, humorous, tested and proven/battle-tested examples make for a very enjoyable and essential read."

—JEFF LEFKOWITZ, author, *Windows to Yesterday* series

"The topics of 'Who,' 'What,' and 'How' of excellent Jewish day schools spring from entertaining narratives filled with exceptional nuance and insider knowledge. The strength of the book lies in the recipes for success that inspire greatness and motivate innovative thinking."

—RABBI SHMUEL FELD, founding director, JEIC—
Jewish Education Innovation Challenge

Raising A+ Human Beings

Crafting a Jewish School Culture of Academic Excellence and AP Kindness

Dr. Bruce Powell
Head Emeritus, de Toledo High School
Distinguished Lecturer of Jewish Education, American Jewish University

Dr. Ron Wolfson
Fingerhut Professor of Education, American Jewish University
Author, *Relational Judaism*

Foreword by **Rabbi Elaine Zecher**
Temple Israel, Boston, MA

Preface by **Rabbi Ed Feinstein**
Valley Beth Shalom, Encino, CA

Raising A+ Human Beings
Crafting a Jewish School Culture of Academic Excellence and AP Kindness

2021 Quality Paperback Edition, Third Printing
© 2021 by Bruce Powell and Ron Wolfson
Foreword © 2021 by Elaine Zecher
Preface © 2021 by Ed Feinstein

The Kripke Institute
Institute for School Culture
5110 Densmore Avenue
Encino, CA 91436
ronwolfson1234@gmail.com

ISBN 978-0-9795483-2-1

First Edition

For
Deborah Strauss Powell
and
Susie Kukawka Wolfson
Our A+ partners in life

CONTENTS

FOREWORD

Rabbi Elaine Zecher

The story goes something like this: There once was a man who lived in Cracow. Each night he had the same dream. Buried under a bridge in Prague lay a treasure. He would awake in the morning startled as if it were really true. Yet he knew that to travel the distance would take great effort. Finally he decided to make the journey. He arrived in Prague but didn't know which way to turn. He happened upon the local wise woman. She saw his confusion and kindly asked him what he was looking for. Tired and yet eager to fulfill his mission, he shared the whole story. She laughed, nodded her head, and gently let him know that she had a similar dream like his but the treasure was actually buried under the stove of a man who looked exactly like him. His eyes lit up with the realization he hadn't considered. He ran all the way back home to discover that the treasure was in his house all along.

When we dream of crafting a culture of kindness, an appreciation for each person's humanity, and engendering meaning and joy within our Jewish institutions, we may regard such discoveries as a long sought-after treasure. Bruce Powell, assisted by Ron Wolfson—both extraordinary educators and human beings—help us turn this dream into reality. They are like the treasure hunter Indiana Jones, who valiantly unearthed priceless treasures. Fortunately, our treasure hunt does not involve snakes. Nevertheless, it is no dream. The treasure has been with us all along. We just needed a map to learn how to uncover the goodness buried within every person's soul and allow it to shape the experience for everyone.

We know this from the beginning of creation, as Powell cites, that every human being is created in the image of the Divine, *b'tzelem Elohim*. In that act of coming into existence, implanted within our souls is how God declares what has been formed: that it is "very good," *tov me'od*. Here lies the simple truth. Goodness is inherent. How do we uncover it and allow it to thrive in any Jewish environment, educational or otherwise?

We need a treasure map—or as Ron Wolfson calls it, a blueprint—applicable not just to Jewish day schools but in every place we gather in the Jewish community. Thoughtful, intentional, proactive, and loving environments have enormous impact that ripples beyond the classroom, sanctuary, and social hall.

Many of us grew up hearing that our report cards go into our permanent record and, in effect, determine our successes and failures in the future. It turns out our permanent record in Judaism is how we ensure grace, loving-kindness, and compassion in the way we regard ourselves and others. Powell and Wolfson take us step by step, through the words and images we employ, with the people we bring into our midst, and in the way we understand how we interact, learn, teach, and grow together.

Maya Angelou, of blessed memory, taught that people forget what you say and do but they never forget how you made them feel. Certainly in a school environment, we want our children to be educated and to achieve academic excellence. Yet if it was only that, would we be truly successful? And it is not just in a school. We learn and excel when the culture around us is rooting for our success and we have an active role to play in the creation of that world.

Rabbi Zusya, a Hasidic rebbe, taught that at the ultimate day of judgment, we won't be asked why we weren't more like Moses in our lives but rather why we weren't more like ourselves. It is not always easy to discover our best selves. We need guides such as teachers, rabbis, cantors, camp counselors, and mentors to help us uncover our goodness. We also need supportive, caring, loving environments that are clear about the culture they seek to create, with a clarity of purpose.

Bruce Powell recognizes that in every interaction, the full community—from the board members to the grandparents to the custodians to the substitute teachers to the faculty and to the students themselves—are all partners in the work to create a culture of kindness and, as Powell calls us, A+ human beings.

We may all dream of discovering a treasure. We do not need to travel far. We each hold that treasure within us. The way to craft a world within our institutions that cherishes and lifts up each person for their goodness is just a few pages away.

Rabbi Elaine Zecher
Temple Israel of Boston
Boston, Massachusetts

PREFACE

Rabbi Ed Feinstein

I appoint you this day
Over nations and kingdoms:
To uproot and to pull down,
to destroy and to overthrow,
to build and to plant.

— JEREMIAH 1:10

I remember my first Parents Night as a head of school:

"Your job is to get my kid into a good college!" a parent informed me.

"All we ask is that you give our kids the tools to be successful!" offered another.

"We expect excellence, and nothing less!"

Education in American culture is perceived as a process of preparation, a bridge from an innocent childhood to a successful adulthood. But what success? Is success in school solely the college degree, the credential that opens to a good job that, in turn, brings material prosperity, security, and prestige? Is that all we want for our children? What of happiness, a sense of moral purpose, the discovery of personal meaning? Are those among the legitimate goals of education?

When they stand before us on the verge of adolescence as a Bar or Bat Mitzvah, we have them read the words of the biblical prophets of the haftarah. The intent of that ritual is more than a demonstration of proficiency in the enunciation of Hebrew phrases. The rite is meant to implant the moral spirit of the prophets into the growing child; to direct the diffuse energies of adolescent rebellion toward the prophetic project of *tikkun*, healing and repairing the world. The Bar/Bat Mitzvah ritual aims to draw the teenager's focus away from the self and all its drama toward the world and all its needs; to give our children the prophet's moral responsibility and moral empowerment. We give them the gift of the prophetic voice. More valuable than any other gift, what the developing teen needs most is a sense of mission, an abiding sense of purpose.

Bruce Powell, beloved educator and winner of the Covenant Award for his brilliant career building Jewish high schools, believes the principal goal of secondary education is the formation of "A+ human beings." School must stand for more than academic excellence. It must impart "AP kindness," a sensitivity for the divine image in each human soul. And, in turn, school must offer a developing young soul a sense of personal significance in a life lived with moral purpose.

Calculus, chemistry, Shakespeare can all be taught from the front of a classroom. Qualities of character are taught in a different way, through a school's culture. In the myriad ways a school community touches a young person's life—the way new students and their families are welcomed into the community, the way teachers and students talk with one another, the way academic achievement is framed for students—a school can cultivate what Powell describes as "the empathic mind." Moral sensibility is taught in the classroom, but even more so in the lunchroom, on the athletic field, in the school boardroom, and in the informal gatherings of students, parents, and teachers. Adds pioneering Jewish educator Ron Wolfson, Powell's friend and muse, enculturation comes from participation—immersion into a culture and its expectations. Wolfson, author and advocate of Relational Judaism, has devoted a career to revealing the powerful ways institutional cultures in synagogues and schools inculcate values.

Rebel Without a Cause, To Sir with Love, Up the Down Staircase, The Breakfast Club, Fast Times at Ridgemont High, Ferris Bueller's Day Off, Clueless, Juno, Lady Bird . . . our culture is obsessed with high school coming-of-age stories. The great mystery of how we pass through the tumultuous teenage years and miraculously emerge as nominally healthy adults fascinates us. Bruce Powell and Ron Wolfson have found the way to make high school a sacred moment of spiritual and moral formation, a time of joyful self-discovery and supportive community. Welcome to a vision of the way high school ought to be for all our children!

Rabbi Ed Feinstein
Valley Beth Shalom
Encino, California

WELCOME

Dr. Ron Wolfson

As a professor of Jewish education at American Jewish University in Los Angeles, I am privileged to teach the next generation of Jewish educators. In my courses, I seek to introduce them to the best principles and practices of the field, often presented to them by guest educators who work on the front lines in Jewish schools, synagogues, and camps. For many years, one of the favorite guests has been Dr. Bruce Powell.

Bruce brings to the students his vast experience as the founder of three extraordinarily successful Jewish day high schools and his vision of how to build a unique school culture infused with deep Jewish values. During his lectures, the instant he talks about shaping "A+ human beings" as the signature goal of his schools, the students lean forward in anticipation of learning the principles of how to create such a culture.

At the end of each of his many outstanding lectures over the years, I would invariably run up to Bruce, thank him profusely, and say, "You must write a book about this." He always replied, "Ron, I'm way too busy *running* the school to *write* about the school." I understood, but I kept asking, knowing that such a book would be an important contribution to the field of Jewish education. The minute I heard Bruce was retiring from his head of school position at de Toledo High School, I called him and said simply, "Now's the time because you'll have the time." He demurred: "I don't know how to write a book. *You* know how to write a book." I offered to mentor Bruce through the process. He then surprised me: "Why don't we write it together, Ron?"

I jumped at the opportunity, not only due to my deep admiration for his outstanding achievements as leader of the phenomenal Jewish day schools he headed and as a sought-after consultant to dozens more day schools throughout the land, but also because Bruce is an A+ human being. He walks his talk, and I am thrilled his "talk" is now in print.

This book is the "Torah of Bruce." It presents a detailed blueprint for building a culture of academic excellence and kindness based on his extraordinary track record building three outstanding Jewish day high schools. This is a manual that can be read and discussed among educational leaders, in faculty meetings, and with boards of directors and parents, with questions at the end of each chapter for considering how you are crafting the culture in your community. It is filled with the best practices Bruce pioneered in his schools, but more importantly, you will discover the best *principles* underlying those practices. You may be lucky enough, like Bruce, to create a culture of academic excellence and kindness from scratch in a new school. Or you may be a new head of school walking into an existing culture seeking to understand it, name it, change it, and shape it. Perhaps you are a board leader concerned about a toxic culture in your school or organization and need a path forward for repairing it. Although the practices are drawn from the setting of a Jewish day school, these principles will be useful for anyone—professional or lay—charged with crafting culture in many of our communal institutions, including supplemental religious schools, synagogues, summer camps, Jewish community centers, Hillels, youth groups, and even your family.

I thank Bruce for inviting me to reflect on these principles by adding my own brief stories about crafting an advanced placement culture of kindness. All the rest is the incredibly practical, immediately applicable, and engagingly written wisdom of my friend and colleague Dr. Bruce Powell.

INTRODUCTION

Dr. Bruce Powell

It was May of 1980. I was the general studies principal at Yeshiva University of Los Angeles High School (YULA). The school is an Orthodox Jewish high school, and I oversaw the general studies programs in math, science, English, history, and languages.

Each morning at the girls campus, the students would have their prayer service, and then we would take some time for announcements. Since it was May, final exams were right around the corner, and I could sense a debilitating tension in the air. The burden of studying for finals was palpable. The seniors had already been admitted to colleges, but the juniors were very much on edge, given the perceived high stakes regarding how colleges would view their eleventh-grade academic records. The tension from the eleventh graders permeated the room, causing subliminal panic among the ninth and tenth graders as well. The girls were a mess of worry and stress.

It was usually my task to close the morning meeting with logistical announcements for the day. That day, however, I recognized that some calming words might be in order, words that would address the tension in the room. Here is what I said:

> Girls, I want to share with you a personal story. In eleventh grade, I received a D in chemistry class. In those days, if you got a D in any major class, the University of California (UCLA) would automatically disqualify you from entering the college. I was desperate to attend UCLA with my friends, and now my hopes were dashed. Indeed, I was

despondent, depressed, and without hope. Years later, I realized that not everyone can be an A student in chemistry but that through good deeds, loyal friendship, and treating others with dignity, I could indeed be an A+ human being.

At this point in my story, I became emotional, and as I recall, my voice was a bit raised. I continued, with some passion and pleading:

> It seems to me that every girl in this room is an A+ human being even if you are not an A+ student in every subject. So, has anyone done a good deed today? Has anyone brought joy to a friend? If so, you are an A+ person, so stop worrying about grades. Study hard, but always know that life and friends will judge you on the grades that do not appear on your transcript. Please be A+ human beings every day.

(By the way, I retook chemistry in twelfth grade. I don't recall my exact scores in the class; I am sure it was a close call. I ended with a C. That fall, I entered UCLA.)

My words seemed to bring a certain calm to the room, and I could feel the tension drain. The girls began to consider their personal behaviors and actions toward others.

As it turned out, that moment became a cultural touchstone for the students of YULA high school. A mantra developed: "Being an A+ human being was of equal or most likely greater importance in life than being an A+ student."

Unaware at the time, I had engendered the beginnings of a school culture of kindness and embrace by reframing words for my students. Years later, as I led de Toledo High School with the help of visionary teachers and dedicated members of the board, I understood the power of words and ideas in creating and reframing culture. Indeed, I learned how important culture can be for children; how it can create perspective and, in the long run, help develop highly successful human beings.

Forty years after that moment in 1980, former students—many of whom became parents of students at de Toledo High School—often recollect to me how the idea of being an A+ human being helped them in their own moments of despair, lost hope, or even momentary depression over some bad outcome. The words became a metaphorical bootstrap by which they could achieve perspective and thereby regain their ability to move forward in a positive manner. These recollections were cemented by an understanding of the importance of a positive and healthful school culture.

Crafting Culture—Ron

While attending college, I learned about crafting culture when I was challenged to shape one as a young novice Jewish educator in St. Louis, Missouri. The rabbi of a large synagogue, B'nai Amoona, hired me to teach in an innovative experimental post–Bar/Bat Mitzvah program. The rabbi, Bernard Lipnick, knew that something had to be done to engage eighth graders—the Vov class—in a manner different from the same Hebrew school model they had before puberty. His idea was as radical as it was simple: bring summer camp into the regular school year by taking the kids on monthly retreats. The class would meet twice a week to prepare for the weekends. But the rabbi needed a youth group/camp counselor type to lead the experiment, and he found me.

At the time, I knew nothing about teaching and certainly even less about shaping innovative school culture, but I had been a leader in United Synagogue Youth (USY). I had rebelled against the culture of the Hebrew school I grew up in, having dropped out immediately after my Bar Mitzvah. USY—and my family—brought me back into Jewish life, and I loved the culture of the youth group.

My first and most important objective was to shape the norms of the group. I began with an emphasis on welcoming. Rather than wait behind a desk in our classroom to greet the fifteen students, I hung out in the lobby of the synagogue building to engage them as soon as they entered. It was there I could hear their stories, share mine, and interact in a way different from the typical teacher-student relationship. The rules of engagement in the classroom had been learned through years of student experience—rules that kicked in the minute we walked into that space. But out in the hall we could act differently, more informally. The objective of this welcoming work was to show the students that I wanted to know them and that I deeply cared about each of them as a human being. As my colleague Harlene Appelman likes to say, "Students don't care how much you know until they know how much you care."

This cultural building block continued into the school and weekend experiences through a series of norms—standards of conduct—that emerged as we shaped our classroom community. I established a check-in time at the beginning of each meeting, inviting the students to share the stories of their lives. And I willingly shared mine. Everyone had two "rights" during any conversation: the right to privacy and the right to say no. I never wanted the kids to feel as though they had to reveal things they wanted to keep to themselves, and I always wanted them to feel in control of what they did or did not participate in. For example, if we explored our emotional responses to a difficult film about the Holocaust, the students could always pass on contributing. Although we held worship services on Shabbat, if a student wanted to sit out on a particular experience, I would allow it, always following up privately to explore why.

These norms led to a school culture in which the students knew they had a cocreating role. They were junior partners in much of the decision-making that guided the class. It was clear that I was in charge, but my charges were always consulted and often given choices about important aspects of the class—what themes we would explore on the weekends, how we would spend our free time on Saturday nights. This created what my professor, the educational psychologist Richard deCharms, termed an *origin climate*, wherein students were encouraged to originate their behavior. The opposite, common in many classrooms, was a culture in which students felt like pawns, mostly powerless and constantly manipulated.

In the end, the combination of curriculum content, learning experiences, and what the philosopher and education reformer John Dewey would call a "democratic" classroom crystallized in a central goal: to create a relational community where the relationships between me and the students and the students and one another were paramount. This led to a superordinate goal for the group, first articulated by one of the students when curious parents near the end of the year asked what was going on in the Vov class: "We are learning to live together." To which I added, "Jewishly—we are learning to live together Jewishly."[1]

de Toledo High School Founding

Fast-forward to the year 2000. I had helped found, develop, and lead two large Jewish day high schools in Los Angeles: YULA (1979–1992) and Milken Community High School (1992–2000). In the spring of 2000, a group of visionary lay leaders approached me to consider heading a new community Jewish high school in Los Angeles. The Greater Los Angeles region already had many excellent public and private high schools, among them the aforementioned schools and perhaps another fourteen Orthodox Jewish high schools of various philosophical leanings.

The enthusiastic community leaders formed into a board of directors for the new school, and they asked me several critical questions:

How would our new enterprise be different?

What would set it apart?

Could we compete head-on with the well-established independent private schools in Los Angeles?

Could we be better than they in sports, or academics, or arts?

How long would it take us to develop a reputation for academic excellence?

Of course, no one believed that a start-up Jewish community high school could achieve such lofty goals as top college admissions, superb academics, performance-level arts, and championship athletics in fewer than twenty years of operations.

So, what could we do in year one that would set us apart?

We all agreed that perhaps the most important thing we could achieve in the first year was to develop a unique school and community culture. I convinced our board that creating top academics, sports, and arts was the easy part of school creation (just hire great teachers and coaches). However, school culture creation posed a much greater challenge.

We all knew what great academics looked like—top AP scores, top college admissions, creative teaching, and motivated students. But what did great school culture look like? How would we know when great school culture was achieved? How could we measure school culture, if at all? There certainly was no "SAT test" for school culture, and colleges didn't ask for students' "grades in school culture" when requesting an academic transcript from the registrar.

Finally, why was creating a special or unique school culture so important for our success? Would it help improve students' grades or test scores? Would it improve our success in college admissions? Who really cared about school culture in the hard-hitting world where tuition-paying parents demanded excellence in all manner of tangible outcomes yet no one was demanding outstanding school culture? Indeed, most people were not even sure what "culture" meant or why it mattered.

The challenge of creating the reason for school culture, and creating the school culture itself, fell to our school's faculty, board, parents, and—of course—our students.

Book Overview

Raising A+ Human Beings is the story of how words and metaphors become reality in the hands of talented educators and dedicated constituents. There is real power in these words and metaphors, power to craft a school culture that informs, motivates, inspires, and shapes character. These metaphors and words include the following:

A+ human beings—the *outcome* of the culture we aim to craft

AP kindness—the advanced placement *course* in which students learn how to be A+ human beings and in which every student is *enrolled* from day one until graduation

Academic excellence—teaching foundational knowledge using a pedagogy that inspires students to lead lives of purpose and meaning

We begin our story with the *what of A+ school culture*—our end goal—in chapter 1. In chapter 2, we consider the *what of values* and how they inform our work. We then turn in chapter 3 to the *who*—the creators of embracing culture; in this case, the culture of a Jewish day school. Chapter 4 is a deep dive into the practical—the *how* culture comes alive. Finally, in chapter 5, we look at parents, grandparents, and families—the critical partners in the work of raising A+ human beings.

While school is the case study, the principles of culture crafting apply across institutions and organizations, even in our families. It may be among the most important things we do for our children and the well-being of our communities.

1

The *What* of A+ School Culture

When we talk about the *what* of a school or institution, we usually mean the program—what the kids or participants do every day. What courses do they take? What extracurricular activities are offered? What do sports look like? Indeed, the *what* is usually a tangible, material thing.

I would imagine that every school offers long lists of whats. Indeed, with few exceptions, top-rated Jewish schools all look pretty much the same. Everyone is offering some version of math, science, English, history, Jewish studies, languages, arts, sports, and so forth.

The same is true for most Jewish institutions, whether they be synagogues, Jewish community centers, Hillels on college campuses, and summer camps. For example, synagogues offer versions of worship services, religious school, adult education, social justice outreach, and so forth.

Here, I am suggesting a new kind of *what* that focuses on fashioning a unique narrative: crafting a school culture of excellence and kindness, creating outstanding human beings, and engendering for the students a meta-meaning and purpose for their academics, arts, and sports. I am also suggesting that language, values, metaphors, and narrative are vital parts of the *what*. We use language and narrative to articulate why we study math and science, why Jewish wisdom is vital, and how all of this is important to a person's life.

We know from life that words and stories often create reality. When we hear negative words about our work, most of us experience some kind of physical reaction within our minds and bodies. Conversely, when we receive compliments about our work, our attitudes brighten, thereby creating a new, tangible reality in our lives. And if our actions become part of the story, the narrative, the very language of a school, we feel enormously empowered.

On a macro level, we know that history is filled with men and women who used words and narrative to alter the reality of millions of people: Judaism gave a book of words and stories to the world that changed the reality of most human civilizations; the words and stories of Jesus and Muhammad engendered material transformations for over three billion people; Karl Marx wrote a small book that literally altered the reality of perhaps one-third of the world. Moreover, words lead to the creation and vision of nations and communities. The philosophical ideals and narratives of Thomas Jefferson, Thomas Paine, Abraham Lincoln, Harriet Beecher Stowe, Elizabeth Cady Stanton, Emma Lazarus, Martin Luther King Jr., and Maya Angelou, among others, helped shape America. Words from Judith Plaskow, Sarah Schenirer, Abraham Joshua Heschel, Joseph B. Soloveitchik, Moses Maimonides, Abraham Isaac Kook, Rashi, Franz Rosenzweig, Mordecai Kaplan, Moses Mendelssohn, and so forth guided the trajectory of Jewish philosophical history over the past thousand years.

In this chapter I will share with you the words, values, and metaphors that created the deeper *what* of de Toledo High School. They are words and metaphors that created a narrative that inspires board members, teachers, and students to greater aspirations of human behavior and interaction. They are words that are used daily in the life of the school, because I believe redundancy is the key to communication. Indeed, these words and ideas are the genesis of culture at de Toledo High School and the driving force behind the *what* of academics and all other programs. If examined carefully, it is powerful words and ideas such as these that ultimately drive the founding cultures and excellence of every great institution.

A+ Human Beings

Teenagers, and even children as young as third grade, continually worry about their grades in school. The concept of a "report card" is deeply embedded in our society, and kids become caught up in this culture of letter grades determining their success and even their self-worth.

The report-card metaphor is used almost daily in our general American culture as well. How many times have we heard "She did A+ work on that audit" or "I give our politicians a C- in fulfilling their campaign pledges." Indeed, some kind of report-card metaphor finds its way into almost every facet of our daily lives.

At de Toledo High School, and at two other high schools I helped develop, we turned the embedded report-card metaphor on its head. Instead of constant promotion of academic grades, we created our own metaphor: in life, it's as important—and usually more important—to be an A+ human being than to be an A+ academic student, because not everyone can be perfect in chemistry but everyone can receive an A in kindness, in doing good deeds, and by contributing to our school community.

This simple reconfiguration of the metaphor, this change of language, engendered widespread relief, reduced stress, clarified the real priorities and values in life, and increased students' motivation to excel in their academic work.

Over time, hundreds of former students have written to me or told me in person how liberating it was for them in high school to know that they were indeed A+ human beings, no matter what it said on their English or math grade. And every one of these alumni has found success in the "real" world of work and family. Most importantly, they have a clear sense of their values, who they are and what they stand for, and what their task is as they sojourn in our world.

When the Fraternity Met Jewish Values—Bruce

Many years ago, a young man graduated from de Toledo High School (then named New Community Jewish High School). He matriculated to an outstanding university where he ultimately pursued medicine, and today he is a practicing physician.

During his undergraduate years, he pledged a fraternity on campus. In the first semester, after being accepted to the fraternity's pledge class, the pledges were subjected to some abusive hazing, the purpose of which was to debase the pledges and diminish their dignity as human beings. He recently explained that at one point in the hazing process, he simply walked out and told the others that what was going on was antithetical to the Jewish and human values he learned in high school. He simply wouldn't stand for it. And remembering that he was an A+ human being would not allow either physical or psychological debasement of that value.

He was ultimately accepted into the fraternity as a full member, and operating from inside the system, he worked to abolish the damaging and debasing hazing process.

AP Kindness

In our highly academic world of independent Jewish and secular private schools, advanced placement courses and high scores on the subsequent AP exams are often seen as the pinnacle of academic success. Students who enroll in ten or twelve AP courses during their high school years often receive great accolades from teachers, fellow students, and especially parents.

In the founding of de Toledo High School, the concept and reality of "advanced placement" became a convenient, well-known, and rich metaphor when applied to other realms of school achievement. Why not advanced placement community service? Or advanced placement humanity?

At de Toledo, we hit upon the metaphor of "advanced placement kindness." We explained to students that whereas not everyone might take AP academic classes, everyone is automatically enrolled in AP kindness; and everyone is expected to receive a top score in this "course" by the time they graduate and employ that kindness throughout their lives.

Relational Kindness—Ron

I am a teacher who believes that our best learning comes from experience. In my book *Relational Judaism*, I suggest that sharing experiences is a foundational element of building a caring, relational community. It is also one of the most important ways we shape our characters. So recently I have been reflecting upon those times when I have been an eyewitness to acts of *chesed* (loving-kindness), moments when one human being shows kindness to another. When we do something for others, we demonstrate the very essence of a relational community.

My late parents, Bernice and Alan (*z"l*), were my first and most important teachers of *chesed*. During an earlier viral pandemic that ravaged the world—polio—they befriended a young woman named Ruby. Like the coronavirus of 2020, polio attacked Ruby's lungs to the point where she could not breathe on her own. Long before ventilators were invented, polio patients were confined to an "iron lung," a long cylindrical negative pressure device that forced air into the lungs. Lying on her back on what was called the "cookie sheet," only Ruby's head stuck out of this respirator. Remarkably, Ruby could read, write, and even run a business. She became the leading seller of Avon products in Omaha, Nebraska. Our family visited Ruby often, bringing her favorite magazines, playing gin rummy, and just schmoozing. When a portable respirator became available, my father would lift Ruby out of the iron lung into a wheelchair and take her to the movies and the theater and for long car rides. She was a lifelong friend.

One day, one of my mother's girlfriends returned from a national Women's League for Conservative Judaism convention, where she had learned about a sisterhood chapter that helped a blind Jewish boy become Bar Mitzvah by transcribing the siddur into Braille. The friend asked my mom, "Do you think, Bernice, we could create a Braille group at Beth El?" To this day, I don't know why this story captured my mother's heart, but it did. She recruited a bunch of her girlfriends, and they commandeered a closet in the basement of the synagogue, raised the money to buy Braille typewriters and fabricating equipment, taught themselves how to transcribe both English and Hebrew, and created the first-ever Passover Haggadah for the blind. The women in the Braille group became lifelong friends.

My father never finished high school. After his father went broke, my dad had to work to help bring in some money for the family. For the rest of his life, he was a voracious reader, teaching himself a vast vocabulary. When he finished a book, he never kept it. He gave it away to those he knew would be interested in the topic. These readers also became his lifelong friends.

At our Passover seder table, Mom and Dad always invited guests. Each year, they would call Offutt Air Force Base to ask if any Jewish soldiers needed an invitation to a seder. Some years, they called Boys Town—the home for at-risk juveniles located just outside the Omaha city limits—to offer Jewish kids a chance to celebrate with us. One of these boys became a lifelong friend, too.

My parents never uttered the word *chesed*. They didn't sit me down to teach me how to live a life of loving-kindness. They did something much, much better. They got me up off the couch and took me with them to visit Ruby, to paste the Braille pages of the Haggadah together, to share a love of reading, to welcome a stranger in need of a place at the table. In each of these experiences, I learned that the reward for this *chesed* was the lifelong relationships they created with all the people whose lives they touched.

May these memories of my parents continue to be a blessing and inspiration to all who are embracing a life of relational kindness.

Circles of Friends

When de Toledo High School first opened in 2002, I taught the new ninth graders that cliques were not allowed at our high school. Rather, I urged the students to have "circles of friends."

A student asked, "What is the difference?"

A clique, I explained, is an insecure group of people who are so afraid of the "other" that they need to keep people out of their group. They want insularity. They are usually selfish and certainly far less secure than those who have open arms.

A circle of friends, on the other hand, is a secure group of people that lets anyone join. There is always one more place at the lunch bench—no one has to fear eating alone at lunch; there is always an extra space at the party. A circle of friends finds ways to embrace, to include, to see the gifts and contributions the "other" can make.

The distinction between circles of friends and cliques created a palpable transformation among the students. After I provided this new metaphor to the group of ninth graders, there was a sense of relief in the room. Of course, most ninth graders are insecure. (In over fifty years in the field, I have rarely encountered a fully secure fourteen-year-old.) The students could use these words and metaphors as a good "excuse" to be friends with everyone. If criticized by a fellow classmate, questioning, "Why is she sitting at our table for lunch?" the student can respond, "Well, aren't we a circle of friends? Stop being so insecure."

Today at de Toledo High School, please visit and witness lunchtime, or any time for that matter. I invite guests to walk around the grassy quad and simply ask the kids, "Who are you?" Invariably they will get a good old teenage eye roll, and the answer will be "We're a circle of friends. Would you like to join us for lunch?"

It is within the eye roll that we know we have been successful. In ninth grade, the students know what they are supposed to say. By grade eleven, they mean it. By grade twelve, it is part of their DNA.

The concept of circles of friends is now a permanent and powerful part of the school culture at de Toledo. The words have been actualized. Whether at lunch, at a party, on a Shabbaton, or when welcoming a guest, students live within the circle.

Imagine the transformation at any school, youth group, or institution if people were to internalize the ideal of circles of friends!

No Gossip (*Lashon Hara*)

A great rabbi commonly referred to as the Chofetz Chaim wrote tractates on our obligations of speech in the Jewish tradition. The rules and laws are many and often complex. For the purpose of building high school culture, the words "No gossip (*lashon hara*)" would have to suffice.

Unlike the relief felt by students upon learning about circles of friends, there were some very curious looks when I taught them that Judaism does not allow us to say anything bad about anyone, to anyone, using any kind of communication whether it be verbal, digital, written, or innuendo.

The skeptical looks were followed by some laughs and responses such as "That's not possible" or "I like to gossip. What else do I have to talk about except other people?" Of course, one student asked, "You mean you never gossip to your wife?"

I explained that I have broken the rules of gossip on numerous occasions over the course of my life, and almost every time two things happen: my words come back to haunt me, and I always feel bad about saying negative words about another human being, even in private. Gossip transforms my soul into something I'd rather not be.

After further explanation, with a rabbi answering questions about the details of what constitutes *lashon hara*, students began to wonder what it might be like to go to a school where they were not afraid that people were talking behind their backs. They began to realize that such change must start with each person making an internal commitment to refrain from *lashon hara*. And in every classroom, the teachers reminded the students of how the "no *lashon hara*" rule would enhance our school culture and create a safe space to learn, grow, debate complex issues, and—most importantly to kids—engender greater friendships.

On an all-school Shabbaton, a twelfth grader overheard some ninth graders speaking harshly about another student. The twelfth grader walked over to the group and said, "We don't do that here." That was the moment we realized that perhaps our school culture had gained some powerful traction.

Academic Excellence

Almost without exception, every parent wants their children to attend a high school that is academically excellent. Most students want to as well.

The challenge, however, is defining "excellence." What does that look like? Is it predominantly high grades among the school's current students? Superior SAT scores? Offering twenty AP courses in which 90 percent of the students score fours and fives? Is it a school with superb and abundant athletic teams? Endless offerings in the arts? A world-class maker space? College-level science labs?

Most parents, students, and educators would all agree that the above list is certainly a good part of what makes for excellence. What is missing, however, is a deeper understanding that *excellence* is a relative term, not an absolute. At its core, *excellence* means to excel—to do better than the national average in areas of measurable accomplishments. Or does it really mean "to excel" beyond what an individual child might think they can achieve?

If, for example, a child enters third grade only able to read Dick-and-Jane-type books and ends third grade reading the Harry Potter series, then we can certainly say they have excelled. But are they excellent? Compared to their reading level in September, the answer is a resounding yes! However, if a child enters third grade already reading the Harry Potter series and by June is still reading at the same level, then can we say they have excelled?

No doubt a third grader who can read all seven volumes of Harry Potter would certainly be regarded as excellent for their grade level. Even when measured on a relative scale against all readers in North America, one can safely say that a third grader who can read the Harry Potter books is an excellent reader.

My argument is that an excellent reader must excel beyond where they began, even if their entry-level skills are excellent on a relative scale to the nation.

The outcome of this kind of thinking about excellence transforms the culture of schools in profound ways. Excellence is now measured by how effective the school is in inspiring children to find their gifts and then excel beyond what they can already do. All excellence is now relative to the gifts of each individual child. Some children have gifts in math and can excel by twelfth grade to taking AP Calculus BC; others are simply solid math students who excel into Algebra II after starting ninth grade in a two-year Algebra I sequence.

At the end of their journeys in math education, both groups feel validated, both have excelled, and both have nurtured their gifts in ways that make sense for them.

Now, when asking the question about whether a school is academically excellent, the answer may be whether or not that school has a culture of excellence where each child's gifts are identified and all students thereby excel well beyond their starting points.

In my experience, this kind of thinking is a relief for parents, kids, and boards. Schools that have rigorous entrance requirements and take only students gifted in math, science, and English may or may not be truly excellent schools.

However, a school that truly engenders a culture of excellence—that admits a wide-range of students, each with unique gifts, and then inspires students to excel beyond their gifts—that school, in my view, is academically excellent in every facet of its program, ethos, and culture. It is also a school where the souls of children are not crushed by some kind of unrealistic striving for an imaginary standard unattainable by many. Rather, it is a school where a student can comfortably say, "I am great at literature and not so good in math, and that's okay. My school will help me soar in literary understanding and provide a solid math background without making me feel inadequate as a human being because math is challenging for me."

An "excellent" school does not pander to the notion that Ivy League college admissions is the only path for higher education. We know it's not. Rather, it promotes a supportive culture where students are inspired to learn based upon their unique gifts and souls.

Every Human Being Is Created in the Image of God

In the biblical creation story, the Torah says, "And God created human beings in God's image . . . male and female, God created them" (Genesis 1:27). I would offer that this simple statement is perhaps the most powerful vision for education ever uttered or written. It is also the foundational concept for building school culture.

At de Toledo High School—and frankly, what should be the aim of every great high school, Jewish, Christian, Muslim, or secular—the notion that our students are created in God's image is interpreted in two ways. First, it means that every child—every human being, for that matter—is of infinite value. Beings of "infinite value" must be treated with kindness and dignity, and they can never encounter embarrassment from teachers or bullying from fellow students. Our school cultures must be rooted in diversity, equity, and inclusion.

Second, if we believe that every student is created in God's image, then we must also hold that every child is endowed with unique gifts. It falls to our educators to help students find and nurture those gifts and fully burnish their divine image.

Imagine a teaching staff that has internalized such a view of children. Imagine a school culture where teachers embrace this concept and actively seek to uncover the special "images" in each of our children.

The Empathic Mind—Bruce

In the early years of creating de Toledo High School, I asked department chairs to write a mission statement for their departments. Most of the statements were solid visions that included thinking skills, content goals, love of learning, an ethos of inquiry, and so forth. Each mission was several sentences in length. I was very pleased with their efforts.

The English department, true to their poetic mindset, submitted its mission in one simple clause: "To create the empathic mind."

In one powerful phrase they had captured the *why* of education and described a profound outcome for our students.

"What," I asked the English teacher Linda Martin, "is the 'empathic mind'?"

The teacher explained that the person with that kind of mind embraces knowledge in its deepest forms, integrates that knowledge into their soul, often transforming their very being. The person with that kind of mind hears and sees what others do not—or cannot. With that kind of mind, they can envision what is not yet there but know that it can be achieved with unified communal efforts. And the person with that kind of mind embraces the ideas and feelings of the "other."

I was quite taken by the thoughts of our English teacher. I shared with her the story of Moses and the burning bush. I explained that perhaps hundreds of people, maybe thousands, had passed by the burning bush in the desert over several millennia, yet none had recognized this strange fire that burned unceasingly. Only Moses seemed to recognize that there was something special, even miraculous, occurring before him.

She stopped my story in midsentence. That's it, she said. Moses had an empathic mind. He embraced the wonder and acted upon it.

The teacher and I communicated our thoughts to the teaching staff over the next several years. By doing so, we taught people what it looks like to inspire and thereby how to create an inspiring culture and empathic minds.

Questions for Crafting Your Culture

1. The key to the *what* of a school is its unique words, metaphors, narrative. What are these at your school, synagogue, supplementary school, youth group, or Jewish Community Center?

2. What are some signs that they resonate with constituents?

3. What is evidence that they are memorable and thereby easy to understand and repeat? How can you make them more so?

4. How might you change or improve words, metaphors, narrative to be more effective?

5. What are indicators that the narrative is working? For recruitment? For fundraising?

6. Describe the deeper *what* within the culture of the school that creates the context and meaning behind everything you do.

2

The *What* of Values

Building positive, creative, caring, values-laden Jewish school culture is a task that requires a deep understanding of Jewish values. It is a primary task in educating A+ human beings. It also requires a language set that articulates a clear understanding of what counts as a value and what counts as a Jewish value and ultimately conveys a vision for how to insert value language and ethos into the thinking of every member of the faculty, board, parent body, and student population.

The following suggests a pathway to clarity on what is, indeed, the distinct nature and contribution of Jewish values and wisdom to our communities and our nation. Most importantly, and for our purposes of creating rich and powerful school or institutional cultures, this section provides a partial vision of the language every educator, parent, board member and student can integrate into their thinking and actions and thereby ultimately transform their cultures.

For easy reference, below is a list of selected values that help create a pathway toward our students becoming A+ human beings (of course, there are dozens more):

- Wisdom
- The Good
- Obligations of Speech
- Justice
- Sacred Community

- Reflective Eating and Blessing
- Meaning of Life
- Joy
- The Root of Religion Is *Lig*
- Humility

Wisdom Completes Education

In our contemporary world, there exists massive amounts of information—often incorrectly regarded as knowledge—and, by extension, enormous potential for power. Google, for example, allows us to access seemingly endless amounts of information, even knowledge, affording many a pathway to power. What Google does not provide is the wisdom of how to use that power for the good.

In the same way, science provides humanity with an almost Godly ability to, among other things, cure disease, repair severed limbs, reconstruct burned faces, and restore health through organ transplants. We certainly regard these advances as wise and good. Yet science also is on the brink of creating human life within a laboratory setting. What wisdom do we need before crossing the cloning threshold? What will be the consequences? What kind of power will our ability to create human life engender? How and who will control such power? Have human beings developed the wisdom to set ethical boundaries on such awesome work?

In Judaism the acquisition of knowledge must be inexorably bound together with the development of wisdom. The combination of knowledge and wisdom forms the basis for greatness in education. Anything less is weak and dangerous. The future of our communities and the world depends upon raising up generations of students who possess deep knowledge *and* deep wisdom.

Now imagine a school that constantly directs its students to seek wisdom—a school that teaches its students to embrace both knowledge and wisdom, that knowledge and wisdom are inseparable. Students then understand that Judaism provides us with the wisdom we need to use knowledge in a moral way.

Moreover, imagine the science, math, and English teachers guiding their students to employ wisdom in the application of their newfound knowledge and power. Imagine that they sojourn in a world composed of their own knowledge and creativity. I believe these students are sure to consult with the timeless wisdom of Jewish culture, texts, and law before bringing to life the results of their knowledge.

PhD and SOB—Bruce

Shlomo Bardin, the founder and long-serving director of the Brandeis-Bardin Institute (now a part of the American Jewish University), used to tell a story about a gathering of Nazis held in Wannsee, a suburb of Berlin, in January 1942, that became known as the Wannsee Conference. The purpose of the conference was to plan the "Final Solution" of the Jews of Europe—in essence, the murder of every Jewish human being on the European continent. Dr. Bardin explained that perhaps 25 percent of the attendees of the conference held master's degrees or doctorates from German universities. He then quipped, "It seems that one can be a PhD and an SOB." He continued to explain that "even a great secular education does not guarantee that one will be a moral human being."

Making Goodness the Goal

On January 15, 2009, Captain Chesley "Sully" Sullenberger III safely landed a US Airways A320 commercial jet aircraft on the Hudson River in New York City after the plane had become disabled by a flock of geese fouling the engines.

Taking emergency actions, Captain Sullenberger saved all 155 passengers and crew. For many, this incident is now known as the "Miracle on the Hudson." In an interview about the incident with news anchor Katie Couric, Sullenberger said, "One way of looking at this might be that for forty-two years, I've been making small, regular deposits in this bank of experience, education, and training. And on January 15, 2009, the balance was sufficient so that I could make a very large withdrawal."[1]

There have been many discussions at all levels of society, business, and government dissecting the elements of Captain Sullenberger's actions. In my view, the answer may be summed up in a piece of wisdom I learned from Rabbi Harold M. Schulweis in 1982.

At a gala dinner to raise money for the Heschel West Day School (now renamed Ilan Ramon Day School) in Agoura, California, Rabbi Schulweis was explaining how he always expected "the best" of his children in whatever they did. He described himself "hovering" over his young son, encouraging him to do his "best." Reflecting back on his child-rearing tactics, he told the audience that whereas he had doggedly focused on the "best," he had failed to combine striving for the "best" with achieving the "good." He then said that today, he now understands that "the best is the enemy of the good."

It seems that Captain Sullenberger had already integrated this axiom many years before. I believe that Sully never believed that he was the "best." What he certainly believes to this day is that we must continue to learn, to enhance our skills, to make "regular deposits" in the "bank of experience" and learning. No deposits were necessary in the "bank of the best." Rather, his "deposits" led to an amazing amount of "good." Just ask the 155 people on that flight how good they feel today.

Now imagine how this concept can be integrated and used within the culture of Jewish schools. What happens if we use Sully's metaphor of "deposits" and suggest to our students that each mitzvah they do, each kindness they engender, adds to their "bank account" of goodness? Imagine the relief among students and parents as they detox from the false measurement foisted upon them by cultures of the "best." Imagine as they move instead toward a culture that seeks the "good," embracing Jewish values as a standard of success in life and understanding that being the "best" at being good is really the goal.

What happens if our language with students—whether studying science, history, or politics—seeks to place everything into the context of the value of goodness?

Can we then say that societies that contribute to democratic ideals are good? Nations that afford their people civil rights and equal access to education are good? Communities that regard all of their inhabitants as equal partners in building societies are good? Nations that strive for economic justice, food security, and intolerance of oppression of any kind are good?

Moreover, how does culture transform when students and parents stop using the term *best*? *Best* is a relative term that ensures that only one person can achieve that title. For example, it can mean, especially in the minds of children, "Since I am not the 'best' in sports, then perhaps I shouldn't even bother playing the game." However, *good* is rarely a relative term. Everyone can be good; indeed, everyone can be great at being good.

In changing our language to "goodness," all our students on their way to becoming A+ human beings can strive to be an *or l'goyim* (light unto the nations; Isaiah 42:6), a light of goodness.

Albert Einstein once quipped, "Any fool can know. The point is to understand." So, too, fools can be the best at knowing, but they may lack the wisdom to transform that knowing into goodness.

Obligations of Speech

In *Words That Hurt, Words That Heal*, Rabbi Joseph Telushkin tells the story of Oliver Sipple, the man who saved the life of President Gerald Ford during an assassination attempt by Sara Jane Moore on September 22, 1975.[2]

Sipple, a decorated Vietnam War veteran and an ex-Marine, was standing near Moore when he heard the first gunshot. She missed. He then grabbed her arm before the second shot was fired, thereby, by many accounts, saving the life of the president. Sipple was regarded as a hero. When questioned about his heroic actions, Sipple demurred and simply told the press that he did what anyone would have done if given the chance.

Shortly after the incident, the press "outed" Sipple, reporting to the world that he was gay. In 1975, before the gay rights movement had really taken root, being gay was a great embarrassment for Sipple's family in

Detroit. The family was teased and hounded by neighbors, and eventually Oliver and his family became estranged. Whereas this estrangement was repaired before Sipple's death from pneumonia in 1989, he ended up suing seven newspapers, losing those suits in 1984. Sipple's question was simply "Why can't I live as I want?"

In most democratic nations, citizens are guaranteed the right to free speech. This right is often regarded as sacred, and it certainly can be argued to be the backbone of democracy. For many, the question is always "What are my rights to speech?" Yet when free speech is filtered through a Jewish values lens, a slightly different and nuanced idea emerges. We ask, "What are our obligations of speech?" Whereas most citizens in democracies cherish freedom of speech, Judaism, along with other religious traditions, demands that we ask ourselves about the limits and the boundaries of that speech.

So, for our students, two questions arise:

- What are we obligated to say?
- What are we obligated not to say?

These are powerful questions that might serve as a foundation for the *what* of school culture. They can certainly serve as part of the road map for our kids on their journey toward becoming A+ human beings.

So now let's imagine our school culture where freedom of speech is linked to obligations of speech—where student newspapers are careful with their words, students do not fear *lashon hara* (gossip), and the internet becomes a "safe space" for kids to communicate without worry, embarrassment, or revelations of personal information that provide no benefit to our society. News is now redefined as something of moral value, of benefit, and something we need to know so as to ensure that we act when injustices are perpetrated in our communities or our world. Speech now becomes a tool for the good. The combination of free speech and obligations of speech creates a radical transformation for human discourse and certainly a radical transformation of the culture of our schools as we actualize the Jewish values of speech.

Justice, Justice You Shall Pursue

To understand and apply the Jewish view of justice within the language and values of our schools, as well as using it as another signpost on the road to creating A+ human beings, it is helpful to examine another view of ethics.

In *Situation Ethics*, Joseph Fletcher defines *agape* as doing that which is the most loving thing at the moment. More broadly, he states that "all laws and rules and principles and ideals and norms are only contingent, only valid if they happen to serve love."[3]

Fletcher's view is based upon what most of us would consider a strong emotion: love. In this case, love might take on the attributes of charity/agape, empathy, compassion, and kindness.

I learned about Fletcher's views while sitting in a graduate seminar class at the University of Southern California in 1974. The professor was extolling the virtues of Fletcher's view. Most of the class participants accepted this view as almost immutable truth. I raised my hand and asked a simple question: "Professor, what happens if a person does not feel loving at any given moment? Does that mean that he would not give a poor person on the street a dollar for food?" In a follow-up question I asked, "What happens if a person believes she is doing what is most loving at the moment, but the receiver of that love does not want it? Or what happens if a society believes that what is most loving is to rid itself of a particular race, oppress a particular ethnic group, or expel a particular people from its midst?"

The professor, coming from a very different ethical tradition, was not sure how to answer the question. A fellow student, Rabbi Reuven Huttler, and I approached the professor after class to explain more fully the Jewish view of *agape*. We reminded the professor that perhaps many Germans during the Nazi era, 1933–1945, believed they were doing what was most loving for Germany by expelling and murdering Jews in Europe. Their putative "love" for the "Fatherland," as distorted by Hitler, led to horrific consequences.

Over the next several weeks, Rabbi Huttler and I explained to both the class and the professor that in Judaism, doing that which is the most loving thing at the moment is not necessarily the best tactic when thinking about ethics. We introduced the idea of *tzedakah*, the Hebrew term often used by Jews in daily parlance to mean "charity," but in reality its meaning is "justice," thereby taking on a vastly different way of thinking.

First, the Jewish idea of justice has an obligatory qualification. Whether or not we "feel" loving at the moment, we are still required to provide help to those in need. *Tzedakah* is not voluntary; it is required. It is based not on an emotion but rather on a profound understanding of Jewish law and tradition, as well as what is needed for a society to achieve justice and fairness. It is even required that the poor give, so as to provide them with the dignity of being one who can also give, not only take. This dignity is a form of justice.

Second, the great twelfth-century Jewish philosopher Moses Maimonides explained that the highest level of *tzedakah* is to teach people a trade so that they will never have to ask for support. Indeed, providing people a pathway toward self-sufficiency is the highest form of justice, for both the society and the individual. This kind of justice leads to dignity and to future contributions by the recipient toward a more complete and just society. The outcome of *tzedakah*, of justice, of an obligation founded upon law, can never be an emotional response. It cannot lead to "loving someone to death." It cannot create emotionally charged situations where entire nations "love" themselves to the exclusion of creating a just society.

Developing the language of justice in our schools—allowing students to grapple with what is just, what counts as just actions, and what is unjust—opens a rich and nuanced dialogue. It becomes another touchstone for our teachers to envision the knowledge they impart as leading to a more just society. It also becomes the underpinnings of student relationships, as they consider a lifelong definition for themselves as being people of justice and how they can channel that understanding toward sustainable ethical actions.

Sacred Community

Many in North America who grew up in the 1950s and '60s remember the iconic television commercials extolling the virtues of smoking Marlboro cigarettes. The "Marlboro Man," mounted on his well-bred yet lean horse, became a symbol for the strong, rugged, independent man: alone on the plains of the great frontiers, a clear vision for the future; a chiseled chin and facial lines that embodied tough experience and wisdom. And, of course, he had a Marlboro cigarette dangling from his mouth, placing the crowning touch on what the company wanted us all to believe was the perfect North American template for manliness.

The commercials were a tremendous success. Seared into the ethos of national culture, and certainly into the minds of young boys, was the clear message that a true "man" did things alone, he was self-sufficient, and, of course, he smoked Marlboros. The commercials were, in many ways, a reflection of what many Americans thought to be the underpinnings of our nation's emerging power and commercial success in the world: America stands tall, we stand alone, we are self-sufficient, and we need no one's help.

The values of Judaism provide a different vision regarding what constitutes a powerful and successful society. In *Pirkei Avot* (Ethics of the Ancestors), Hillel implores us, "Do not separate yourself from the community" (*Avot* 2:5). Hillel's axiom, written about two thousand years ago, reflects biblical thinking and the contemporary wisdom of the rabbis of the Mishnaic period, circa 50 BCE. It promotes a vision for the individual and for the nation. Hillel also asks, "If I am not for myself, who will be for me? But if I am only for myself, what am I? And if not now, when?" (*Avot* 1:14). Here, Hillel understands that, at times, we advocate for ourselves, and yet by doing so, we must also ask, "Who will be for me?" If I only advocate for myself, this will surely alienate me from others. Hillel then asks an existential question by indicating that if "I am only for myself, what am I?" In other words, I can barely exist standing alone; indeed, this is an impossible state of being. And finally, when action is called for, especially in a time that demands justice, action must be taken now, and it must be done as a community.

Unlike the rugged individualists enshrined by the Marlboro Man, the Jewish vision understands that only through interaction with and full participation in community may a person find meaning, purpose, and—to

put it in modern psychological parlance—self-actualization. Even from
the very beginning of the biblical story of Adam, God says that "it is not
good for a human to be alone" (Genesis 2:18). It is within this value of
community that a very different story emerges for Jewish life and for a far
more powerful vision for our greater community.

Imagine the culture of a school where the mindset of the students is
one that demands that we place the well-being of our community ahead
of our individual needs. It used to be this way—as a rule, not the exception. Today, selfless acts seem to always make the news: a man runs into
a burning home to save a stranger; a woman returns money she finds in a
desk she purchased at a swap meet to the rightful owner; a family takes in
a homeless child without asking for anything in return (this one was made
into the movie *The Blind Side*); an anonymous man hands out hundreds of
ten-dollar bills to homeless people during the Christmas season; a young
woman, not yet twelve years old, runs a national campaign to raise money
to cure a rare disease. Why aren't these actions the norm? Why do they
make news?

In a school where the culture of community takes precedence over the
culture of individualism, these stories become the norm. Students realize
that no one becomes successful alone. Rather, we stand on the shoulders of
those who came before us. We stand on the shoulders of the community.

Born on Third Base—Bruce

During a Shabbat exposition of the week's Torah portion, Rabbi
Edward Feinstein of Valley Beth Shalom in Encino, California,
made the following comment: "Some people who were born on
third base believe that they had hit a triple." In this brief and certainly humorous observation, Rabbi Feinstein drives home the
point that no one can claim he or she achieves success without the
foundations built before they arrived on Earth. Someone found
the land to build the field; others graded the field and made it
useful for baseball; others still provided the bases, the bats, the
training, and, for that matter, created the game itself. All of these

efforts were done by communities of visionary and hard-working people who wanted to ensure a great future for their children. Many of us and our students were lucky enough to have been born on "third base."

Reflective Eating and Blessings

My father-in-law, Dr. Ludwig Strauss (*z"l*), was fond of describing physicians at a major Los Angeles hospital rushing up the stairs to their next appointment while eating their lunches literally "on the run." Being one of the more senior members of the medical community, he would stop them and simply say, "Doctor, heal thyself."

In our society today, doing things "on the run" is best reflected by the unique invention of fast food. Waiting is a lost art; we must have it *now*. In most cities and towns, large or small, we see lines of cars outside fast-food establishments. People order their food by speaker system, receive their meals through the windows of their cars, and often proceed to eat their meals as they drive to their next appointments. Little or no time is given to appreciating the meal, proper digestion, or enjoyment of the moment. Instead, we demand fast food for our fast and often overburdened lives. Fast food has become a metaphor for lives lived in haste.

Judaism, along with its sister religions, offers a different cultural and values paradigm. Instead of fast food, it offers the value of "reflective eating." In traditional Judaism, we are obligated to say one hundred blessings each day. At least six of those blessings involve meals. We must say a blessing before and after we eat. Of course, these blessings thank God for the food we eat, and they encourage a moment of self-reflection regarding how that food arrived on our tables, or, for that matter, in our cars.

In 1985, while serving as director of the Brandeis Collegiate Institute in Simi Valley California, Rabbi Donniel Hartman gave a lecture about the importance of Shabbat. He likened it to a "speed bump" in the week to slow us down, reflect, and enjoy Shabbat as characterized by Abraham Joshua Heschel as "a palace in time."[4]

Over time, I realized that blessings serve the same purpose as Shabbat. They act as "speed bumps" during the course of our day. When we sit down for a meal, instead of digging in, we pause, say a blessing, perhaps reflect upon what it takes on the part of the farmer, the truckers, the markets, the food preparers, the utensil makers, and Mother Nature to create that meal and bring it to our tables. By saying blessings, we move from fast food to reflective eating and certainly to appreciation. Perhaps that single shift in behavior is transformative well beyond just eating a meal?

Expanding the metaphor of fast food and reflective eating to the next level, to the notion of saying one hundred blessings each day, we begin a change from fast living to reflective lives. In Judaism, there are blessings for almost every action and for the many wonders we encounter daily. We bless the washing of our hands, for example. We recognize the power of water to rejuvenate, cleanse, prevent disease, and prepare us to eat "bread." We make a blessing on thunder and lightning, on rainbows, on the beginning of a new month, upon eating seasonal fruit for the first time that year, upon all new beginnings, upon opening our eyes in the morning, upon marveling at the wonders of the body after using the restroom, and the list goes on and on. At every turn, blessings slow us down. We feel those gentle "speed bumps" in life's road that remind us to take nothing for granted.

In recent years, there has been a movement to create "mindfulness," especially for children in our schools. It is a powerful movement that helps people focus on and appreciate the moment. Reciting one hundred blessings each day is perhaps the ultimate in mindful behavior, using the concrete recitation of blessings to continually focus our souls, minds, and bodies toward self-reflection, appreciation, and the simple joy of being alive.

Moreover, blessings engender humility. They remind us that the land we live on and the bodies we inhabit are "on loan" to us and must be returned in good shape. Blessings also elevate our actions to the realm of the sacred. Fast food often debases the action of eating to an animallike function of self-preservation. There is no joy or meaning in such action; there is simply sustenance without appreciation, reflection, or understanding of the intricate life forces that sustain our world. Blessings transform fast-food culture to a culture where we begin to achieve a complete understanding of how intricate and delicate the ecology of life really is. Blessings ritualize mindfulness. They bring acute awareness, sharpen our senses, create an organic rhythm to living, and keep us grounded and humble as we acknowledge the constant wonders of creation.

Now imagine shaping a school culture toward the rhythms of reflection, of "slow food," of appreciation. I believe these values are additional building blocks in the culture that shapes A+ human beings.

Meaning, Not Measuring, of Life

In 1930, at the Faculty Club of Columbia University in New York City, the thirty-one-year-old future Jewish educator Shlomo Bardin from Palestine was asked to present a lecture in his field of doctoral study: education. He explained to the assembled professors that he was disturbed by the shallow goals of American education. He had observed during his sojourn in New York that American education seemed to be focused on "measuring." At every turn, students were tested on their knowledge and skills. He rarely saw time for reflection, deep understanding, and the higher-order thinking skills of analysis, synthesis, and evaluation.

More to the point, he rarely if ever saw an emphasis on perhaps the highest-order thinking skill of all: determining meaning. When were the students guided to explore the existential questions about life? How might teachers imbue their subject matter with layers of unseen meaning? How might they communicate to their students that the dates and circumstances for the outbreak of World War II are not to be remembered for a test but rather to use as a touchpoint for how people view the nature of modern warfare and how it alters our view of the nature of humanity's cruelty? Or how Hamlet's soliloquy "To be or not to be" is not for the purpose of simple recitation or superficial analysis but rather as a prompt to examine the very nature of our humanity? Or how might the study of Einstein's theory of relativity not serve as the subject of a mind-bending test question but rather as a powerful insight for how students view the very nature of physical reality? Or how all of this knowledge forms a template for students to determine how to launch their own search for personal meaning and purpose in a world where such a search is fraught with difficulty and confusion?

At that Faculty Club lecture in 1930, Shlomo Bardin challenged the very nature of how education is done in America. His challenge resonates to our modern day. Over ninety years since Bardin's lecture, America continues to "measure." Indeed, we have elevated measuring to a high art and an economic juggernaut. Testing companies reap millions of dollars to develop and administer tests such as the ACT, SAT, ERB, Iowa, CAT, ISEE, GRE, LSAT, GMAT, AP—the alphabet-soup of test names goes on and on. Teachers teach to the tests, rarely pausing to ascertain meaning in their subjects. Test-prep companies reap millions proving that, for the right price, they will ensure high scores on standardized tests, thereby opening doors to the top universities. And teachers are pressured to succeed as "measured" by inorganic exams that have no bearing on how a student might succeed in college. (All the research indicates that high school grades are, in fact, the best indicator of future college success.) Programs such as No Child Left Behind and Race to the Top are noble yet flawed attempts to promote success in our nation's public schools because success is measured, once again, by standardized test scores.

And we wonder why schools are failing. We wonder why students become bored with their studies. We wonder why testing is simply not working to promote real achievement.

What we do know is that when a subject feels real to a child, the child becomes interested and generally excels. We use the word *relevance* as the pathway for how to connect to kids; perhaps focusing on how a subject may engender meaning for young minds is an effective path to relevance. Perhaps the mission for education should simply be "to engender in students meaning so as to lead meaningful lives of contribution to our world." Race to the Top now redefines the "top" as a life of meaning and purpose; No Child Left Behind now means that no children are left behind without developing a vision of contribution for their lives. Once these macro goals are understood and integrated into an educational system and culture, then knowledge and skills become essential and even interesting tools for students to achieve the goal of meaning. The new goal of "engendering meaning" becomes a powerful motivator rather than reliance on the disincentives of "testing and forgetting." Once acquired, meaning is rarely forgotten.

I believe that in 1930, Shlomo Bardin had it right. I also believe that the soul of the great Western experiment in democracy depends upon a deliberate move away from measuring and toward embracing the notion of educating for meaning. Meaning is a powerful motivator. It leads to creativity, joy in learning, and a passion for learning that must be mastered so as to infuse that meaning with substance and depth. Such a value shift from measuring to meaning truly moves a nation from mediocre to a meta vision for education and a macro vision for a nation's contribution to our world. Meaning is certainly one of the powerful *what*s of our schools' cultures.

Joy: The Enduring Emotion

In 1955, my parents packed up our Chevy station wagon and we traveled two hours from the San Fernando Valley in Los Angeles to the city of Anaheim, California. A new family-oriented theme park had just opened, and having been raised on Mickey Mouse since birth, we were beyond excited to meet him in person at what was to become the world-famous Disneyland.

Upon driving into the parking lot, we saw for the first time the famous sign over the entrance: "The Happiest Place on Earth." Over the sixty-five-plus years since then, I have been back to Disneyland many times. I was there for "Grad Nite" from high school; I was there as a new father sharing the wonders of the place with my young children; and now my wife and I plan to bring our grandkids to the park and experience its wonders once again through the eyes of children. For many, Disneyland is indeed the "happiest place on Earth."

Returning home from a Disneyland excursion, wearing our Mickey Mouse ears, the "happiness" seemed to quickly fade away. Similar to sweet candy—or, in my case, chocolate cake—the taste lingers for a while and then slips into faded memory. In fact, many times, by the time we returned home from Disneyland, I was no longer "happy." And by the second week we were home, the Mickey ears were broken and seemed to disappear into the next day's trash pickup. Whereas Disneyland was certainly fun for the moment, it had no long-lasting impact. It changed a few hours of our lives, but then was gone.

In July 1977, my wife and I experienced the birth of our daughter, the first of four children. We wanted to celebrate her birth with a home-based naming ceremony, and those were the days when creative thinkers were developing Jewish birth ceremonies for girls that reflected the *brit* (covenant) ceremony performed for Jewish boys. We put together a ceremony called *Simchat Bat* (the joy of the daughter). At the end of this ceremony, attended by family and friends and including the Talmudic mandate to plant a tree for each girl (and use the future branches to support the chuppah [wedding canopy] at her wedding), I realized that I did not feel happy, so to speak, but I felt a much deeper emotion. I understood at that moment the concept of *simcha* (joy).

Unlike happiness (and Disneyland), joy is an emotion that seems to last forever. It is an emotion that becomes embedded in our DNA. It is a moment that alters our worldview. It colors how we experience work, friends, and connectedness with others. Joy becomes a lifestyle that engenders meaning.

I realized at my daughter's *Simchat Bat* that the difference between happiness and joy is that joy is happiness with meaningful purpose and long-lasting implications for life. Our home that day was, indeed, the most joyful (and meaningful) place on Earth.

A few weeks after the ceremony, and now moving into the rhythm of day-to-day child-rearing, bill paying, commuting to work, and nonstop worrying about child safety devices, I began to wonder if the joy we felt that day was momentary or long-lasting. What had we really done?

In 1999, our daughter called us from college and told us she was engaged to be married. I had a year to save up for the wedding—and thank God our future son-in-law's parents offered to pay half. The year of planning for the wedding was exciting, often daunting, and certainly filled with emotion and, yes, joy.

The wedding occurred in 2000, on a Sunday afternoon. We spent the weekend immediately prior to the Sunday ceremony together with our new family at camp, sharing a joyful Shabbat together and being amazed that our "babies" were getting married.

At the conclusion of the wedding festivities late Sunday afternoon, I felt a joy that was far beyond anything I had remembered when our first daughter was born. I tried to understand the difference between the *Simchat Bat* and the *Simchat Kiddushin* (joy of the holiness of the wedding). What had changed? What had happened during those twenty-three years to increase my joy so intensely?

The answer was simple: Unlike her birth, this time we had worked very hard to raise a young woman with vision, integrity, good judgment, and values. The increased joy was not an accident; it was earned.

As an educator over the past fifty-plus years, I have met thousands of students and parents. I have heard thousands of times from both that "I just want to be happy" or "I just want my child to be happy." I explain to them that although school may not be the "happiest place on Earth," it is a sacred space where children, and by extension parents, can achieve joy. As I discovered with the birth of our first child and her wedding years later, real and permanent joy must be earned.

All of us remember with various levels of disdain those teachers who made life too easy for us; we "earned" an easy A and thereby felt we cheated the system and the system cheated us. On the other hand, those teachers who challenged us, albeit with competence and kindness; who forced us to earn our grades; who respected us by demanding thoughtful, intelligent, and rigorous assignments—in those classes we achieved real joy of accomplishment. We remember those teachers as having positively transformed our lives. And the joy of learning remains with us throughout our lives, having an impact on every aspect of our work and our vision for living. Unlike the vacuous nature of momentary happiness, joy is a product of earned success, with purpose and meaning.

In our schools, perhaps we can change the conversation by changing the aspirations of both children and parents. Let's replace the statements of "I just want to be happy" and "I just want my child to be happy" to "I want to live joyfully with meaning and purpose" and "I want my children to live joyfully with vision and integrity," all of which they have earned, thereby ensuring that the joy is real and permanent.

The Root of Religion Is *Lig*

In 2006, as part of de Toledo High School's Los Angeles–Tel Aviv partnership program, I met with four Israeli mothers visiting the Israeli students who were part of our exchange program. While sitting in my office, I asked them if they were religious. They all emphatically exclaimed that they were secular and definitely not religious. I then proceeded to ask them what they say to their friends during the days just prior to Yom Kippur. All four of the women said they greet their friends with the Hebrew words g'*mar chatimah tovah* (the implication of this phrase is "May God write a good signature for you in the Book of Life"). They were even a bit confused that I would ask such a simple question. They asked me, "Don't all Jews greet each other with such words before the holiest day of the Jewish year?"

Digging a bit deeper, I asked them who they believed was actually writing a "signature" in the Book of Life. They simultaneously all pointed upward and said, "*HaShem*" (literally, "the Name," an expression usually used by Orthodox Jews who believe that they are not allowed to say any form of the name of God). I asked, "Where does *HaShem* reside when signing the Book of Life, when determining who will live and who will die?" They emphatically responded, "*Bashamayim*, in heaven." I then reviewed with them what they believed—that God was sitting in heaven and deciding who would live and die in the coming year, and then writing God's signature in the Book of Life next to the name of each person. They unanimously agreed that my summary accurately reflected their views.

I then explained to them that in my school's community, if one holds such a belief they would be considered deeply religious, perhaps Orthodox, and certainly not *hiloni* (secular). Once again, they insisted that they were secular and not at all religious.

Of course, what was happening with my Israeli guests was a cultural disconnect based on custom, language, and culture. Their common idiom did not translate for them into "religious" language. For them, it was simply a part of Jewish culture; it was how they communicated with friends and family. It was simply what they said before Yom Kippur without the weight of religion-based language.

During this wonderful and sometimes humorous exchange in my less-than-stellar Hebrew and their limited English, it occurred to me to reexamine the word *religious* to determine if I was missing some level of understanding of the term. As any good former English teacher might do, I looked at the *Oxford English Dictionary*'s definition of the word and found that the root of *religious* is *lig*, meaning "to attach" or "to bind."

This revelation (please excuse the pun) transformed the way I understood *religious*. If we were to remove for a moment the *re* (referring to God) and simply characterize a Jewish person as *ligious*, then everything that happened with the Israeli moms, as well as what happens for many Jews, begins to make complete sense. Most Jews feel "ligious," or connected, to their Judaism. For many, that connectedness may take many forms—Hebrew language, Jewish culture, Jewish values, peoplehood, Israel, food, holiday celebrations, Shoah, Jewish history, familial celebrations, tribal pride, reading a Jewish newspaper, scanning the secular news for Jewish names or Israel-based items, being on JDate, going on Birthright to Israel. The list goes on and on. Of course, even for many secular Jews, as was the case for our "secular" Israeli moms, it also means connectedness to God.

Given this expanded understanding or broad definition of *religious*, I propose that those who reside in the non-Orthodox Jewish world make it a goal to reclaim the word *religious*. Those who send their children to Jewish day schools or camps, for example, can say, "I am religious." Those who support Israel, give *tzedakah*, or have their children play in a Jewish baseball league that meets on Sundays can now say, "I am religious." Those who identify with the Jewish people, who feel pain when they hear about a tragedy in the world and understand that that pain emanates from deeply, even unconsciously held Jewish values, can now say, "I am religious." And if saying that causes discomfort and feels in any way disingenuous, then simply say, "I am Jewishly 'ligious'"—that is, "I am deeply connected to my

Jewish roots, my history, my traditions, my Jewish worldview and values, and my traditional homeland of Israel."

There is no doubt in my mind—or in the research done by Pew—that most Jews are, indeed, connected. As Jewish educators, being "ligious" is a serious statement of who we are for our students. Embracing the *what* of "ligious," of deep connection, allows us to create, thrive, and maintain our unique, meaningful, and particularistic contribution to human history. This sense of connection, this sense of "re*lig*iosity," now allows even the most skeptical students to feel connected and thereby become contributing members of the community in their unique way.

The Grammar of Humility

Most people understand the value of science. Even the most religious people, even if they do not accept certain scientific principles, such as the theory of evolution, still employ the wondrous scientific advances of our civilization. Most rely on medical discoveries to save lives; almost everyone uses a cell phone or owns a computer. Many of the most observant Jews use online resources to enhance the learning of Jewish texts or to answer questions about the finer points of Jewish law.

Indeed, few can argue with the fact that scientific advances have increased our longevity, discovered more healthful ways to live, vastly expanded our food supplies to stave off massive starvation (thanks to Norman Borlaug, among others), helped us to communicate more efficiently, and yes, made warfare deadlier. It has also led, in many cases, to increased polluting of our natural resources. Of course, science is also trying to solve that challenge. With the exception of a rare few, most of the world has embraced science as a marvelous tool for human advancement.

All that said, as an educator, I would like to caution against turning science into a system of dogmatic beliefs. Similar to unbending orthodoxies in religious or political ideologies, absolute "faith" in science may lead to horrendous outcomes. We know from history the brutal and deadly nature of religious absolutes that have led to the murders of those whose religious beliefs do not align with the dominant religious forces.

James Carroll's *Constantine's Sword* describes in painful detail over sixteen hundred years of oppression instituted by the Catholic Church against the Jews in Europe. Today, radical Islam follows a similar path against both Jews and Christians. And Buddhists in Myanmar follow the same oppressive path against the Muslims. The stories of religious orthodoxies oppressing the "other" seem endless.

In the same way, blind faith in political ideologies has had the same result. Faith in communism as the saving path for the former Soviet Union led to the murder of millions by Stalin and Lenin. So, too, blind faith in the orthodoxy of national socialism (Nazism) in Germany or fascism in Italy brought upon the world the deadliest conflict in human history.

I believe a similar blind "faith" in scientific orthodoxies—or more aptly, the misuse of science—may also lead to destructive ends. Back in the 1700s, for example, it was accepted "medical science" that "bleeding" a patient to remove disease, fever, or any number of maladies was the absolute correct path to curing a patient. Belief in that orthodoxy led to many unnecessary deaths.

In a different vein, belief in the science of eugenics, a widespread truism back in the 1920s and beyond, eventually led to the murder of over eleven million innocent souls by the Nazis under the guise that genetic inferiority must be rooted out of the gene pool to allow a super race (read German Aryans) to emerge, untainted by the blood of Jews, gypsies, Catholics, Communists, gays, cripples, and anyone else the Nazis deemed undesirable by using their "scientific" truth.

There are many who believe that science can and will solve almost all humanity's maladies. I suggest that we, as educational and institutional leaders, teach our students or constituents to balance faith in science with a heavy dose of humility. I call this the "grammar of humility."

Grammar simply refers to the internal structures of language and ideas that help humans ascertain meaning. The grammar of humility describes a process and structure of thought that shapes the way we might view the world. Such humility might include taking nothing for granted; questioning every new "truth"; never believing that we are sure we have the absolute correct answer; always harboring some level of internal doubt;

seeking wisdom, not absolute surety; searching for meaning, not simple answers to complex problems; structuring our daily system of thinking—or the grammar of our minds, if you will—so as to become seekers of "truth" while ensuring that our "system of grammar" does not allow for hubris and dangerous orthodoxies. In essence, the grammar of humility encourages a restructuring of how we engage in human discourse, how we regard the "other," and how we regard the outcomes of our discourse and thinking. It is a dialectical model that leads not to absolute Truth (as one might imagine Hegel's dialectic) but rather a process that leads to humility about how best to direct the next steps in our progress.

Building such a grammar of humility into the cultures of our schools and institutions may go a long way toward engendering respectful dialogue and disagreement, openness to the views of others, and acceptance of views and people who are different from us, and demanding that we carefully examine our assumptions as we carefully construct educational pathways for our students.

Perhaps the opposite of humility may be summed up by the American businessman Dan Peña: "I may be wrong, but I'm never in doubt."

Relational Judaism Goes to School—Ron

"It's all about relationships." In 2013, I wrote these words in my book *Relational Judaism: Using the Power of Relationships to Transform the Jewish Community* (Jewish Lights). As we just learned, language is powerful in shaping institutional culture, and the idea of "Relational Judaism" is an example of this in action, now evident in many Jewish organizations that work to build and deepen relationships.

"It's all about relationships" is a truism in schools as well. I like to think about five tiers of relationship that are critical in shaping a relational school culture: (1) between the school and the students and their families, (2) between the students and their friends, (3) between the students and Judaism itself, (4) between the members of the faculty and staff, and (5) between the parents of the school. Let's look at each tier briefly.

1. The greatest compliment a teacher can hear is when a student says, "She's *my* teacher!" I am a big believer in teachers practicing "personal disclosure," the willingness to bring their whole lives to the classroom, to share personal stories, even to invite kids into their homes. When the kids proudly wear swag, they are proclaiming to the world, "This is *my* school!" Teachers who regularly communicate with parents through photos of their kids doing projects and messages, encourage parent participation in learning and volunteering, and even teach parents about subject matter at back-to-school events build relationships with the home. The parent-school partnership is a critical relationship in raising children to be A+ human beings.

2. When the culture of the school encourages the creation of "circles of friends," the message is that relationships among the students themselves are at the very core of a relational community. How does one create a friendship? By sharing one another's stories, by sharing experiences together, by learning and doing together.

3. As the kids study and experience the depth and beauty of Judaism, they build a lifelong relationship with the people, ideas, beliefs, and practices of a religion that will lead them on a path of meaning (what life is all about), purpose ("What am I to do with my God-given talents and passions?"), belonging (a connection to a supportive community), and blessing (a sense that life is filled with sacred moments to be celebrated and elevated).

4. Creating a relational culture in the school is not just important for the students; it is essential that the adults are in relationship as well. The opportunities for faculty members and staff to know one another as human beings; to share their stories; to celebrate their successes and to support one another when things go wrong; to be collaborative, collegial, and caring—these are critical components of crafting the school community. Taking time to check in with each other during faculty meetings, to go away on retreat, to offer "good and welfare," to mark birthdays and anniversaries of service to the school, to help each other with advice, to practice AP

kindness, to be a large circle of friends—these are all strategies for strengthening relationships among the faculty and staff.

5. Parent-to-parent relationships are another critical dimension of the school culture, both to stimulate parental involvement in the school and to network parents together as they navigate the extraordinary experience of raising kids. Think of how you might create "small groups" of parents in your school to foster these relationships. Parents share all four ways of creating small groups of support: (1) affinity—they have kids in the same grade; (2) demography—they usually are in the same stage of life; (3) geography—they often live within the same neighborhoods, sharing carpools and such; (4) availability—as busy as they are, parents can be recruited to volunteer their time, talent, and resources to the school. Reimagine your board, parent-teacher organizations, and parent volunteer committees as "small groups" who not only do the work of the school but also spend time in meetings getting to know each other personally. When the parents connect with one another, they benefit, their kids benefit, and the school benefits. To explore best principles and practices of small groups and other relational strategies, see my book with coauthors Rabbi Nicole Auerbach and Rabbi Lydia Medwin: *The Relational Judaism Handbook: How to Create a Relational Engagement Campaign to Build and Deepen Relationships in Your Community* (Kripke Institute).

Questions for Crafting Your Culture

1. How do Jewish and secular values in your school integrate and interact?

2. How are your students taught the difference between secular or universal values and Jewish values?

3. How does understanding the distinction between a Jewish and secular vision factor into the overall education of your students?

4. How might understanding Jewish and secular values and visions engender a stronger social contract with the Jewish community and national community?

5. How do your students express their appreciation for the value of both Jewish and secular visions?

6. What would our society look like if there were a full integration of both the secular and the Jewish visions? Or does this already exist?

7. What is the language your school uses to focus on core values such as wisdom, goodness, obligations of speech, justice, and so forth?

3

The *Who*

Creators of Embracing School Culture

The Story of the *Who*

I love Nordstrom. Whenever I shop there, the sales staff is always accommodating and helpful. I never have to look for someone to serve me. The piano is often playing in the background, creating a wonderful ambiance. Indeed, if I'm ever in a bad mood, I just go to Nordstrom and wander around; there is always someone to talk to who will brighten my mood. And, of course, I then end up buying a very expensive suit.

What does this story have to do with creating school culture?

Everything!

In the summer of 2002, before we officially opened our doors at de Toledo High School, I had this idea to call Nordstrom in Woodland Hills, California, and ask them to do some pro bono work for our new school located in their local community.

As expected, a delightful person answered the phone and was more than willing to help us. I explained that I'd like the store to send over to our school, only two miles away, the person who trains their sales staff. I thought it would be great to have their trainer provide a short course in customer service to our teachers, office staff, marketing team, and advancement personnel.

The delightful person on the phone explained, with a smile in her voice, that they do not employ a person to train their staff beyond learning how to process a sale on the store computer.

To my complete befuddlement, I asked her how it was possible for the salespeople to be so excellent without any training. How did they know to be so accommodating and kind?

She explained in one sentence: "We hire people who are already like that."

That simple answer set in motion an entire hiring philosophy at de Toledo High School. Indeed, it was the first step in creating the kind and accommodating culture for which the school is well known.

My task over the next eighteen years of school creation and operations was to find people "who were already like that."

The next step was to determine for the school what the "that" looked like. We came up with four basic criteria to screen all potential members of our educational and support teams. All personnel had to:

- Know their subject—yes, know how to answer the phone, raise money, or create a student recruitment plan; or possess a deep knowledge of English, Torah, math, Hebrew, history, and so forth.
- Be able to teach their subject—know how to teach science, for example, and know how to teach kids to treat everyone with respect. This includes those working in the office, cleaning restrooms, or parking cars. It also means that the teacher lives the school's values and has the ability to communicate those values in an inspiring way.
- Love teenagers—not always an easy task as teens traverse those delicate years.
- Have a great sense of humor—in other words, think teens are funny.

Of course, there were several other "thats" that I wanted the *whos* to possess.

First, everyone had to be a "camp-type" person.

One of the signature moments for the school is the all-school retreat—called a Shabbaton, or Sabbath retreat. This is the moment when all four hundred students, seventy faculty members and their families, office staff, and support staff—perhaps five hundred people in all—assemble for three nights and four days at a local retreat center called the Brandeis-Bardin Institute of the American Jewish University, in Simi Valley, California.

Before I understood the importance of who to hire, I often encountered a good deal of pushback from some disgruntled faculty members who had no desire to spend three nights away from their homes. I realized, in good Nordstrom fashion, that I needed to hire people who were camp types—that is, people who already intuitively understood the educational and cultural importance of spending informal time with students. They needed to understand the concept of liminal space, a notion that "forever education" often occurs between the lines—"when you lie down and when you get up" (Deuteronomy 6:7, recited in the daily Jewish prayers). In other words, I had to hire people who were already like that. And that is exactly what we did.

When planning our Shabbaton today, we almost run out of adult housing for our faculty, staff, and their families, since so many people clamor to sign up early to sleep overnight, even though they are only required to be at camp during the daytime programs. (It should be noted that "camp" is only a twenty- to forty-five-minute commute for our faculty from anywhere in Los Angeles.)

Second, and in a similar way, we had to hire people who loved attending student events, whether the prom, sporting events, arts evenings, or science colloquia. Once again, we began to hire people who "were already like that," and these people cemented the school's culture of staff and faculty participation without any contractual requirement to do so.

And finally, we had to hire people with passion for what they do. They had to see education in all of its facets as a calling; they had to regard school as a sacred space where kids can be kids, thereby allowing children to grow into an understanding of their unique gifts. They had to be people who see education not as a job we do but as a life we lead.

Today, de Toledo High School has a team of people who are, indeed, "already like that." And that translates into powerful school culture.

Jack Kennedy and the Janitor—Bruce

There is a famous story widely told about a visit to NASA by President John F. Kennedy.

It was 1962, just at the dawn of America's space age. A year before, President Kennedy had promised, in soaring language in his inaugural address, that Americans would reach the moon before the end of the 1960s.

As the president began his tour of the NASA facility, he noticed a man standing in the building with a broom and dust bin. The president approached the man and said, "Hi, I'm Jack Kennedy. What is your job here?"

"Well, Mr. President," the janitor responded, "I'm helping put a man on the moon."[1]

Of course, the moral of the story is that everyone at NASA understood the ultimate *why* of their work—that they were the essential *who* that would collectively make it happen. No job was too small. All the people at NASA had a hand in eventually helping to land Neil Armstrong, Buzz Aldrin, and Michael Collins on the moon. And on July 20, 1969, they did exactly that.

"We the People"

Let's now take a look at the essential who of our schools—all the people and how they help to create a culture of kindness and to put our kids "on the educational moon."

The Teachers: Inspiring Lifelong Learning

We all know the biblical story of the creation of humankind in the Garden of Eden. God takes what appears to be a worthless lump of clay, shapes it into the likeness of a human being, and then breathes air into the "mouth" of the clod. Miraculously, the clod becomes Adam, the first human.

In Hebrew, the word for "breath" is *nishima*. The root of this word in Hebrew letters is *nun-shin-mem*, or N-Sh-M. The breath, or *nishima*, of God, when shared with Adam, is then transformed into *neshama*, or the human "soul." Notice that the root of both words is exactly the same—N-Sh-M. The vowels, however, are slightly changed.

That slight change of vowels is what I call "inspiration," which in Latin literally means "breathing into." In essence, in went the breath and out came the soul. At that moment, Adam became a human being with awareness and the ability to create meaning through conscious actions.

At that moment, Adam became a unique being.

Indeed, the ability to create meaning through conscious actions is one definition of *inspiration*, which is certainly a core task of our teachers. A teacher's every word is a form of breath. And each breath, each word, must possess a variety of vowel structures and sounds. If a child does not understand the teacher's first set of spoken words, then the teacher changes the words, the nuance, the "vowels," and does so five hundred times, if need be, until the child understands and learns. Of course, our students are certainly far from clods of dirt. They are each on a unique journey toward forming their soul, finding their passions, and learning how to "breathe in" the wonders of their surrounding world.

A group of inspiring teachers thereby becomes the foundation stone of an A+ school culture. These teachers are forever clamoring to discover new sounds, new grammar, new ways of breathing, new pedagogies that provide indelible pathways and skills for lifetime learning.

Teachers Supporting the Head of School—Bruce

Erica Rothblum is the head of school at Pressman Academy in Los Angeles. She tells the following story of how the culture of community was actualized at her school.

One of our school's core values is *kehillah* (community). We talk often about how we explicitly teach kids to live in community as part of our curriculum. We discuss how we—teachers, staff, parents, kids—support one another in good times and in hard times. And so when things were hard in a life cycle (a death or an illness), we expected people to show up. But I was struck by another time when the value of community played out. It was the 2018–19 school year. We had an interim Judaic studies principal, so I was already in a principal search, and our general studies principal, who had been on the job for fourteen months, let me know she was leaving for a head-of-school position in Texas. It was a huge blow to me and to the staff. I did everything I could to show a brave face for the teachers, to be the leader, to tell them we would be okay. After the announcement, a few of the teachers came to my office. I braced myself, expecting a litany of complaints and concerns, and my job would be to reassure them. Instead, they came to tell me that they were there for me, that they knew this was not easy for me, and that I should call upon them if I needed their help. It was a pivotal moment for me to understand how our value of community played out in many different contexts.

The Office Staff: Front Line of Kindness

The tasks of our office staff are usually transactional: answer the phone, pay the bills, send out invoices, create transcripts, process incoming tuition, format letters for the faculty and administration, and perform the myriad tasks necessary to ensure a professional and efficient office operation. At first blush, they do not appear to have an impact on school culture.

Of course, those of us who have worked in schools for more than five minutes understand the vital role a positive office staff plays in generating high morale, positive school ethos, and an embracing culture.

Imagine the relief of nervous and anxious parents who miss a tuition payment and then receive a gentle and soothing phone call from the finance office asking if they need extra time or if there is some problem that the school can help solve. Imagine the smile on the faces of those parents, the reduction in stress, and the increase in those families' love for the school.

Now picture the rushing and hassled parent who enters the school office on her way to work. Her child has forgotten to bring an important assignment due today. The front-desk person calmly tells the parent not to worry; she will personally deliver the assignment to the classroom and all will be well. The rest of the day, the parent feels appreciative, relieved, and relaxed, and she has nothing but great things to say about how the school embraced her worry with no judgment, just kindness.

These two scenarios, which happen daily in schools, are culture-creation moments fully in the hands of the office staff. They are often make-or-break events for the well-being of students and parents. They are both material and symbolic gestures that define a positive school culture.

Calling the School—Bruce

Back in the 1980s, in my work at Yeshiva University of Los Angeles High School, there were many occasions when I phoned Jewish high schools in New York City to inquire about their policies or curriculum.

When placing one of my calls, I was greeted with, "Hello, Yeshiva."

I asked, "Which yeshiva?"

(The word *yeshiva* is a generic term usually meaning an Orthodox Jewish school. In New York, there are perhaps several hundred *yeshivot*, yet each one has a unique name.)

Once the annoyed receptionist clarified that I had the correct yeshiva, I asked if I could speak with the principal.

"He's not here." (And then silence.)

Then I asked, "May I leave a message?"

"Sure." (And then silence.)

Needless to say, the office culture of that school needed some work.

The Receptionist and School Culture—Bruce

Michael Brooks was the long-serving and now retired director of Hillel at the University of Michigan. (Hillel serves as the center for Jewish student life on hundreds of college campuses.) When I think "out-of-the-box thinker," Michael always comes to mind. Indeed, for Michael, there never was a box at all.

One day, many years ago, Michael called his receptionist into his office. Needless to say, when the boss calls you in for no apparent reason, a nervous office worker might think they are being fired.

Michael had other ideas. He extolled her magnificent work in the front office. He explained that she was the finest receptionist he had ever encountered.

Michael told her that she would now have a new title: director of first impressions.

At that moment, Michael created a culture of appreciation in his front office. He symbolically and tangibly acknowledged the importance of those people with whom we have first contact when entering any office or institution. The receptionist's view of her work was elevated. She understood that she was part of the foundation for the ethos and culture of embrace that became the hallmark of Hillel's welcoming culture at the University of Michigan.

"Spiritual Service"—Ron

At Saddleback Church in Orange County, California, Pastor Rick Warren has created a caring culture informed by the best practices of outstanding quality-service organizations and his own understanding of "service" in a spiritual community. Through a sophisticated socialization process delivered in a series of four new-member seminars, those aspiring to be members of Saddleback are not only taught the norms of the congregation but also encouraged to discover their passions and talents—their "spiritual gifts." For example, one person may have the gift of organization, and another the gift of welcoming, and another the gift of direction. Once a person's gift is identified, they seek a volunteer opportunity that can use their gift in building the community. So, the person good at organization might volunteer to organize the thousands of small groups meeting weekly; the welcoming person might become a greeter at six worship services every weekend; and the person good at direction might become a traffic monitor during the busy moments when thousands of people enter the one-hundred-acre campus.

This sounds like basic customer service, but the special sauce at Saddleback is what Pastor Warren preaches about volunteering. Like the Blues Brothers, he teaches his volunteers, "You are on a mission from God." He and his colleagues continually elevate customer service to "spiritual service." Volunteers feel that whatever they do, even something as seemingly menial as emptying the trash or directing traffic, is "God's work." In this way, everyone discovers their own "ministry," their own way of bringing their unique talents to the work of creating the spiritual community.

Identifying personal strengths and matching them to important tasks, elevating the work to "sacred mission," and celebrating success are key components of an advanced placement culture of kindness.

The Board: Indispensable Partners in Crafting Culture

Schools often underestimate the power of the board to create culture. For most, including the board members themselves, the board is some amorphous mass whose purpose is unknown to teachers, parents, and students. Internally, a B+ board will see its task as support for all school operations, policy creation, and selection of the head of school.

However, an A+ board understands its deeper role in school culture creation and exercises exceptional cultural power. Some examples:

- Over the years, under the cultural leadership of Elana Rimmon Zimmerman, the de Toledo High School Board created a special orientation and installation ceremony for new members. New members are provided the usual stuff in the form of a board notebook filled with policies, procedures, recent minutes, and so forth. Toward the end of the orientation, each new member is presented with a de Toledo tallit (prayer shawl). (These tallitot are the same ones given to each graduate before the graduation ceremony.) The prayer for wrapping oneself in the tallit is then recited as the new member dons the tallit. Elana slowly recites the blessing in Hebrew, word for word, so that those unfamiliar with the blessing can easily follow her lead. In this way, no one is embarrassed by their lack of Hebrew skills.

- The board orientation, usually occurring in May, is then followed by the official new-member installation ceremony in June at the home of the board president. Here, once again, each new member is publicly presented with their tallit. All members then join together with their new colleagues to chant the *Shehecheyanu* prayer (a blessing of appreciation for allowing us to reach this special moment. Needless to say, poignant rituals at poignant moments establish indelible cultural moments and memories.

- Each year, on a Saturday night in June, a board member hosts at their home our annual "Havdalah and Dessert" event, where we welcome new parents to the high school. (*Havdalah* means "separation," and it serves to separate the Sabbath from the rest of the week and as a symbolic separation of eighth-grade parents from their children's middle schools and the beginning of the enculturation process into their new high school.) The schmooze time before the Havdalah involves all of the teachers and administrators "working the room," offering warm, welcoming words to the new parents. Parent Organization members also attend, and everyone has on name badges, including the new parents with the names and grades of their children. At the Havdalah ceremony, the head of school and school rabbi offer words of welcome and explanation. The ceremony is then followed by more schmoozing and most everyone leaves by 11 p.m.

- At the opening of school every September, the board chair speaks to the students, offering welcome and inspiration for the upcoming school term.
- Board members often arrange a board visitation day at the school, so they can gain an inside view of the school they so lovingly support.
- Our graduation-ceremony organizers invite the board members to wear caps and gowns and to march with the students in the opening processional.
- At every turn possible, yet without intrusion, the board is "seen" by students and parents. This "seeing" becomes another foundation stone in the construction of an advanced placement culture of kindness.
- The board also creates its own relational culture. Every meeting begins with a *d'var Torah* (an exposition on some salient passages from the Torah), presented by a student or board member. Next, a faculty member presents information about an academic department or important school program. At the end of the meeting, the board president invites each member to share some "good and welfare." These comments range from personal reports about family happenings to information about upcoming community events. They often evolve into statements of appreciation for what the school has "done for their child." People leave the meeting uplifted and look forward to spending time with one another at the next meeting.

Welcoming the New Head of School with Song—Bruce

In 2016, I gave the de Toledo High School Board notice that I would be stepping down from my founding headship in June 2018. I had "lived" the school for eighteen years, I was turning seventy, and it was time to step aside.

After a two-year process, the board selected Mark Shpall, the long-serving dean of students, to be the second head of school. The final vote took place at an evening board meeting in May 2017. The meeting ended around 9:30 p.m. Our founding board chair, Howard Farber, had suggested to me that after the vote, the board travel to Mark's home, knock on his door, and surprise him with a Hebrew song of welcome.

And that's exactly what happened. Board members piled into their cars and drove to the Shpall home, about ten minutes away from the school's campus. We quietly assembled in front of their home and prepared to sing.

We rang the doorbell, and Mark opened the door. He and his wife, Tammy Shpall, our long-serving ninth-grade dean, were overwhelmed with joy when witnessing fifteen board members standing on their front porch, singing a song of welcome.

The story of the board's actions spread far and wide in our community. My guess is that no new head of school had ever received such a welcome in the history of head-of-school hiring in our nation.

The message to our students and parents was clear: we are a school of celebration, warmth, embrace, Jewish values, and welcome.

It was a signature cultural moment.

The Parents: Empowerment, Not Entitlement

In a school of four hundred students, we realized we had access to seven to eight hundred parents and perhaps sixteen hundred grandparents who could also become makers of culture. Our school's culture of embrace—rather than accommodation or toleration of parents—promoted a huge cultural win. By welcoming parents into the building as volunteers, asking them to serve as parent ambassadors at open houses, allowing them to give school tours, nurturing an active Parent Organization (assigning our principal as the chief liaison), and making parents partners in their children's education and moral development, we engendered parent empowerment, not entitlement.

This empowerment led to creative parent initiatives. They understood that we valued their advice, input, and work. In turn, they valued us for valuing them. And out of this process developed a sustainable, visionary, and deeply active parent culture that has swept over our school in the most beneficial ways.

The school also provides special ritual moments for parents.

It is the custom of the school to present each graduating senior with a specially designed school tallit, complete with the school logo, slogan, and a myriad of symbolic design features created by our artist-in-residence, Benny Ferdman. One of those features, found on every tallit, is the tzitzit, specially tied knots attached to the four corners of the tallit.

Around March each year, the parents of seniors are invited to the school to complete the tallit-creation process by tying the knots of the tzitzit. Several parents and at least one board member are present to teach parents how to tie and affix the knots to the tallitot. Whereas the tzitzit are traditionally a reminder of the 613 commandments required of Jewish adults, they now take on the added symbolic weight of parents both physically and symbolically passing on to their children this symbol of lifetime responsibilities. For parents, the act of affixing the knots is deeply emotional.

In June, about thirty minutes before the graduation itself, all seniors, faculty, and parents gather outside the gym in a private spot away from the one thousand guests entering the gym for the graduation ceremony. The entire class stands in a circle. Parents stand behind their child with the customized tallit in hand. Our school rabbi then directs the parents to place the tallit on the shoulders of their graduate, say the blessing, and give their kids a "farewell" hug before starting the processional. This moment is rife with cultural power, filled with meaning. It elevates the graduation moment far beyond the typical high school ceremony to one of sacred space. Needless to say, there are no dry eyes among the moms and dads.

The Student Store—Bruce

One of the benefits of parent involvement was the development of the student store at de Toledo.

In 2013, de Toledo High School moved into its new campus, one hundred thousand square feet in two buildings on five acres.

Beth Gindy and Jeri Cohen, two veteran parents, approached our principal and me and suggested the creation of a student store located in a small space near the new gym in the back building on the campus. We appreciated their initiative and gave them the green light to move forward.

Never did we imagine what would develop from this simple idea. We figured we would make a few dollars to enhance some programs and everyone would go home happy. But we were in for a huge and wonderful surprise.

The store, named the Lipsett Family Jag Shack, started small. Beth and Jeri recruited a few parents to staff the store, and they began by selling some snack food and spirit wear.

By the second year, the store was hosting seventy-five volunteers, in teams of five, working four 2-hour shifts from 10 a.m. to 4 p.m. daily (ending at 1 p.m. on Fridays). And if there was an athletic event in the pool or gym, a match in the wrestling room, or a dance rehearsal in the dance room, the volunteers kept the store open until 6 p.m.

By 2018, the store was grossing $130,000 a year by selling light lunches and a large variety of student-generated needs. The store's surplus paid for a batting cage on the campus, auditorium curtains, lighting and sound equipment for our theater, furniture for our upper and lower lobbies, and a myriad of other improvements to the school's facilities. In aggregate, the store provided well in excess of $200,000 of net support over its first six years of operation.

But, most importantly, it welcomed in seventy-five parents each week who experienced firsthand the vibrant student culture. The parents enhanced that culture with their outstanding work with students in nurturing kindness and offering to help kids when needed.

Today, the Lipsett Family Jag Shack is a central engine of the school's advanced placement culture of community. It is a spot where student, parent, and faculty ethos merge with unsiloed, well-integrated cultural benefits.

And whereas the school cannot claim to "hire" parents who are already "like that," it can claim it created a culture where like-minded parents, attracted to this inclusive culture, choose to congregate.

The Students: Living Kindness in Real Time

High school students—frankly, students of any age—are especially skilled at creating an advanced placement culture of kindness. They engender insider language and reference points. They share memories, humor, and drama unknown by faculty and parents. And given permission by teachers and administration, they offer up the most creative ideas for shaping the unique ethos of the school. The key here, however, is that "permission" to offer up new ideas and act upon those ideas must be an explicit and valued part of the school's vision and macro-cultural milieu. The system for students to engage with administration and faculty should be an integral and encouraged part of school structure.

A Moment When Culture Meets Action—Bruce

The student culture at de Toledo High School is one of inclusion, embrace, and rejection of *lashon hara* (evil speech or gossip). It is important to students that this culture be actualized in real time, not just "feel good" words.

On Friday nights of the school's signature, all-school yearly retreat, the Shabbaton, students gather together by grade level after dinner for a special *Oneg Shabbat* (time of joy). These programs, led by students and teachers, are designed to address the developmental stages of the students. For example, grade twelve sits in a circle in a large room with a large ball of yarn. The strands are passed around to each senior, who then has a chance to thank fellow students or teachers for helping them along their four-year journey or to simply say something important to their class.

For the ninth graders, the program resembles more of a speed-dating session, where students get to know one another and then sit in a circle to share special attributes about fellow classmates. By the time the Shabbaton takes place, ninth graders have experienced about six months of the school's culture of embrace and no *lashon hara*.

On one particular Friday night at the ninth-grade *oneg*, in the middle of the sharing circle, one of the less-mature students blurted out that Andrew (not his real name) was gay. No one knew this fact, nor was Andrew ready to "come out," since he had not even told his parents yet. (This story occurred in 2005, when "coming out" was less accepted in our society. The blurter's words at that point in history were construed to be hurtful and even damaging. This may still be the case in many societies.) At the moment the words left his mouth, ninety-nine pairs of eyes bore in on the blurter, both in support of Andrew and in hard judgment of the blurter. The blurter realized he had made a painful error and ran out of the room in tears. What followed next was the moment of actualization of the school's culture of kindness and embrace.

Ten students went outside to comfort the blurter and help him figure out a way to make amends to Andrew. The rest of the students who remained inside surrounded Andrew in a group hug. No words were necessary. Andrew knew he was home and that his next three high school years would be ones of complete acceptance and joy.

The blurter reentered the room, approached Andrew with a downtrodden face, and apologized. Andrew, who now knew he had everyone's support, found it in his heart to forgive and embrace the blurter. The room was, let's say, a puddle of tears.

Andrew and the blurter became friends, and the school's culture won the moment—a moment and lesson all of these fourteen-year-olds would take with them through life.

At their ten-year high school reunion, this group of men and women shared an unbreakable bond, forged within the culture and values of high school and tested daily during their sojourn through college, military service, business, graduate schools, and future partnerships.

The Security Staff: Balancing Watchfulness and Welcome

Often overlooked when we think about a culture of embrace in our schools is the security staff. In our current world of worry and anxiety about school safety, the security guards stand as both a material and a symbolic statement to parents and children—don't worry, the school is prepared.

That said, the security staff is far more than simply a group of men and women who guard our kids. In most schools, they are the first people seen by the public as they drive into the parking lot or enter the school building.

These security professionals must balance creating a perception of no-nonsense safety while offering friendly greetings to students, parents, and guests. This is no easy task, and it's a job that might be the first stop in promoting the school's culture of kindness and embrace.

The trick is, of course, to project friendliness and embrace with centurion-like, cold-eyed watchfulness. How can this be done?

What we have learned from almost all security professionals is that human intelligence is far more important than guns for the safety of our children. This means that the guards recognize all of the usual constituents—kids, parents, board members, regular guests, volunteers, faculty, and so forth. Better yet, our guards know the names of our children, faculty, and parents. They recognize their cars. By being greeted by name as they drive or walk onto the school campus, everyone feels a sense of welcome—and a sense that since the guards know our names, they also know who should not be here.

In a phrase, the security staff not only "open the doors" of the school building but, more importantly, to the school's culture of caring and safety.

Welcoming and Security—Ron

I am often asked if there is an inherent contradiction between welcoming and security. Nothing could be further from the truth. In many Jewish organizations, the very first face of the institution is the security guard. These professionals are trained to screen people, search bags, and watch for suspicious activity. But in the best of places, the guards are also taught to be greeters, offering a warm "Shabbat shalom" even as they do their work of protecting us. In fact, in many institutions, the security guards are among the most beloved people in the organization. At de Toledo High School, every staff member has learned that she or he is an ambassador of the school, even, especially, the security guards.

The Person Who Guards Me Knows My Name—Bruce

Recently I had the opportunity to visit the Melvin J. Berman Hebrew Academy, located in Rockville, Maryland, near Washington, DC, about which I had heard many great things but had never seen in person. It was a damp, slightly drizzly day as my taxi dropped me off in front of the building. Upon entering the school, I observed—with some level of amazement—a man, Mr. Bill, sitting behind a counter greeting every single child by his or her first name. (The school hosted about six hundred kids.)

Invariably he engaged the students in conversation, inquiring about their weekend or asking specifically about an event he knew they had attended on Sunday. In essence, Mr. Bill knew the kids well beyond their names.

When he saw me, he said, "Oh, you must be Dr. Powell here to visit the rabbi. I'll get him for you."

Mr. Bill had no gun. What he did have was "humint" (human intelligence)—that careful eye that knows when things are in or out of place. I assume he also had a panic switch under his countertop, ready to call the police with a simple push of the button, if needed.

At the moment of my greeting, I felt the culture of the school. I encountered its warm embrace while marveling at how that embrace merged with a powerful sense of security. The remainder of my visit reinforced that the culture was real, even palpable on the part of the office staff, teachers, and students.

In my own city of Los Angeles, the Pressman Academy is located on a major thoroughfare, and is constantly busy with traffic and sidewalk activity. To access the school building, one must enter through a locked gate. Outside the gate stands the security guard. He is decked out in full uniform, prominent weapon on his hip, bulletproof vest on his torso, and a variety of other security tools on his belt. Indeed, when seeing him, people feel secure in believing he can handle any emergency.

However, what the students see every day is not his weaponry but rather a welcoming smile; what they hear is their names as he opens the gate for them; and what they feel is a sense of joy that Joe (not his real name) knows them and that somehow that quick morning encounter sets the tone for what promises to be a good day.

Where There's a Will—Ron

Will Pernell's official title at Stephen Wise Temple is transportation coordinator. The synagogue hosts a large early childhood center, a religious school, and a day school. The campus is situated on the top of a mountain on Mulholland Drive in the Santa Monica Mountains of Los Angeles, and there are only three lanes on the street leading up to the buildings, with very limited parking space. Will is responsible for the smooth flow of traffic in and out of the campus. But he does much more than that; he is a major influencer on the culture of the institution.

Every day, Will stations himself at the drop-off spot, warmly greeting students and parents with grace and humor. Amazingly, he knows all the students by name, welcoming them with a personal word, a fist bump, a high five, an encouragement—"Have a good day!" When asked why he does this, he answers, "My mom. My mom taught me to greet everyone with a smile. It might make their day!"

When I met with the board of the temple, I was told that Will is perhaps the most beloved person in the entire institution. Why? His unbridled enthusiasm for welcoming each and every person he encounters. He is a magnificent model and cultural touchstone for the school and synagogue community.

Watch a video of Will in action, produced by Rabbi Ron Stern, at this link: kripkeinstitute.org/will or https://youtu.be /QnzCMMsBuLg.

The Maintenance Staff: Embodying Kindness and Dignity

Earlier I told the story of the maintenance man at NASA: when asked by President Kennedy what his job was, the janitor said, "To put a man on the moon."

This vision is a signature moment for the school's culture of purpose. The men and women who clean the restrooms, sweep the floors after lunch, clean the classrooms after school, deliver desks and supplies as needed, and reliably lend helping hands can be powerful purveyors of the school's culture. If properly educated and inspired within the school's culture, every maintenance person understands that by ensuring a beautiful campus, everyone feels welcome and cared for. Students learn better in clean classrooms. Guests often judge a school by the tidiness of the restrooms. Teachers appreciate dust-free desks.

Indeed, the maintenance staff's job is to make everyone feel valued because of the embracing physical environment. Their mission is clear, worthwhile, and meaningful. And because of the importance of their work and the dignity by which they are regarded by students and faculty, these men and women acquire nobility of purpose.

Discovery of the Time Capsule—Bruce

Rogelio Salvatierra was the chief maintenance man at an all-girls Yeshiva University of Los Angeles High School where I served as the general studies principal for thirteen years. He knew the names of every student, greeted everyone with a smile as they entered the building, and took great pride in his work.

The school was located in a repurposed building that Rogelio helped to maintain, often with duct tape and strong glue.

One day, Rogelio came running to me and, in an excited voice, explained that he had found an odd plaque embedded in the concrete floor of the maintenance supply room. He noticed that the writing on the plaque was in Hebrew letters. (Yes, he knew it was Hebrew even though he spoke only English and Spanish.) He decided it must be important and called me into his space to determine what it said.

To my amazement, the Hebrew letters were actually spelling Yiddish words. It read, "The Arbiter Ring." Lo and behold, Rogelio had discovered that the building was originally the headquarters for the Workmen's Circle (now the Workers Circle), a Yiddish-speaking organization that promoted the dignity of work. The plaque was dated 1945.

Rogelio, being part of the school's culture of embrace, had recognized he had discovered something of importance to Jewish heritage. He somehow knew in his soul that this plaque was part of the Jewish history of Los Angeles. As it turned out, the plaque was the cover of a time capsule. We never opened it.

Years later, I returned to the school for a visit with my eldest daughter, a graduate of the school. Rogelio greeted us both by name, and we enjoyed remembering the time he found the now-famous plaque on his floor.

In ways large and small, Rogelio was part of the cultural soul of the school. And it is within that soul—and by extension, within his work—children learn, grow, and succeed.

Today, Rogelio continues to educate our children at Yeshiva University of Los Angeles High School.

Honoring Staff—Ron

One day, my mother called me to rave about "the best event in the history of Beth El Synagogue," my home congregation in Omaha, Nebraska. She regaled me with the details: more than five hundred in attendance, incredibly moving tributes about the honoree, over-the-top food, a truly festive feeling in the congregational social hall. I couldn't wait to ask her who the event celebrated, thinking it must have been for the long-serving rabbi, or cantor, or executive director. No, my mother reported. The luncheon was in honor of Lucille White, the cook at the synagogue for thirty-five years. Lucy, as everyone called her, a deeply Christian woman, had prepared the Shabbat luncheons and dinners, baked her famous chocolate chip brownies, and built relationships over the years with nearly every person in the congregation. She had helped us celebrate Bar/Bat Mitzvahs, weddings, baby namings, and countless other life-cycle moments, all with good humor, elegance, and devotion. Most of the speeches had the same theme: Lucy is a member of our family. When they asked Lucy what she wanted as a gift, she shocked the leadership: "I want a leaf on the Tree of Life dedication wall of the congregation." They gave her a branch.

The Donors: Engendering a Philanthropic Culture

Donors know that capital projects are important. They joyfully fund buildings and programs. They take pride in attaching their names to the facility. They like helping kids in need. But, in my experience, donors do not always realize their impact in shaping and sustaining school culture, and we educators often fail to let them know of their importance in this domain.

I recognized that their philanthropy might greatly increase, gain far more meaning, and engender constant joy if donors understood deeply the power they exercised in shaping amazing physical and spiritual spaces for our children or providing ample tuition assistance for those who cannot afford the high cost of an independent school.

Donors are certainly existential to a school's material well-being. They can also be a huge support in creating and sustaining the school's soul.

The Power of Ritual—Bruce

In 2010, when the name of our school was New Community Jewish High School, we decided to invite our board members and other special guests to join the all-school Shabbaton (retreat) to witness and join the school's special Havdalah ceremony and observe the talent show that takes place directly following Havdalah.

Whereas we thought it might be a good way to educate our board about the spirit of the school, we could never have imagined the power of these visits and the transformative nature of the school's culture upon these supportive adults.

When Alyce and Phil de Toledo joined the school's board in 2010, they understood their obligations to provide the three *w*'s of boardship: wisdom, work, and wealth. To this end, when invited to the school's Shabbaton, they cleared their calendars and, along with three or four other board members, joined us for the Saturday-night Havdalah followed by the student talent show.

The Havdalah ceremony is held outside, under the stars. Students stand in four concentric circles. A fifth circle is reserved for faculty and board members.

Alyce and Phil stood in the fifth circle with some faculty and alumni who served as counselors, carefully watching what unfolded before them. They saw the head of school, principal, twelfth- and eleventh-grade deans, and music director standing in the center of four concentric circles of students and faculty. They witnessed the lighting of the Havdalah candle, from which the leadership staff lit single candles and passed the fire on to the twelfth-graders, all of whom were holding single white candles. The seniors then turned and lit single candles held by the juniors standing directly behind them. Groups of three or four students formed Havdalah-candle integrated wicks, and together the entire school chanted the Havdalah service.

Phil and Alyce were overwhelmed by this scene. They had served on other private school boards and had been at many school events. However, they had never witnessed the soul of a school writ large upon the tears of senior and junior boys and girls as they passed the torches of leadership, embraced one another in spirit and body, and thereby passed along the school's cultural aspirations to every ninth- and tenth-grade student.

This moment was then followed by an uplifting talent show around a roaring campfire, with students sitting in the camp's amphitheater. Phil and Alyce were transfixed by the embracing cheers received by every student act. Some were outstanding, some were whimsical, and some needed some polish. Yet the students, with full hearts and joy, seized the moment to actualize the school's value of "advanced placement kindness" through their cheers and warm embrace of all.

Alyce and Phil attended the Shabbaton three more times.

In 2014, after a finance committee meeting where Phil served as chair, Phil and Alyce asked me and the board president, Scott Zimmerman, to remain for a chat. The four of us sat down together, joined by their son, Ben, who was then a senior at the high school.

They handed us a document outlining the parameters of a gift they planned to give to the high school. They were unabashed in explaining to us that the gift was a direct result of witnessing our school's culture of joy and kindness at the Shabbaton, of wanting to preserve that culture, and of thankfulness for having become part of the family that created the culture.

Two months later, the board accepted their gift, and in 2015, the school was officially renamed de Toledo High School in their honor.

Alyce and Phil de Toledo subsequently became even more involved in enhancing the culture that so powerfully embraced them as parents. Today, every fiber of the school reflects their largesse, and the school has become the vessel that holds those values and culture so precious to Alyce and Phil.

Friendraising—Ron

The best fundraisers I've known emphasized the two essentials of effective development work: fundraising as "friendraising" and "show the product." When a school immerses parents and donors in the life of the community and they see the impact of the culture of excellence and kindness on their own children and grandchildren, raising money beyond tuition improves. And with donors like Alyce and Phil, building personal relationships with them, hanging out with them, learning about and caring for their families—these are successful strategies in cultivating donors who will be there for the school long after their own children and grandchildren have graduated.

The Buildings and Offices Are Also the *Who*

In 2014, when we began our renovation project of an existing Jewish Community Center and Federation building, we realized the names of many previous donors adorned almost every wall in the one hundred thousand square feet of buildings. The board and administration decided to preserve every donor name in the building, even though our purchase contract allowed us to remove all but two names. Today, there is a beautiful plaque—more a piece of art—that adorns the outside of our campus even before you walk in the door. On that very large plaque are perhaps two hundred names of those who came before us, upon whose shoulders we stand to this day. The plaque is part of the *who* of our culture of appreciation. It resonates with appreciation and history.

A school's buildings and offices are part of the *who* of a school's culture. Culture creation begins not only with the first greeting from the security guard or the receptionist in the front office. The building itself, in both material and symbolic ways, sends an important message.

Upon entering the lobby of any school, what do we see? What are the cultural messages that the school sends in both subtle and overt ways? Is there student art on the walls? Is there a donor wall? What kinds of photos or banners or electronic messages scroll across the big screen in the lobby? Is there a Hebrew inscription of any kind? Is it translated into English? Is the school's mission easily seen? As I learned from former board member Bryan Palbaum, a top leader for the grocery store company Trader Joe's, "Everything matters, every time."

Each school has a powerful opportunity to express its culture with care and intentionality and with the school's values and mission at the forefront of all displays, colors, words, and even the placement of offices. Below are some examples of how offices and placement send a message and create culture.

The Head-of-School Office: First Impressions

At de Toledo High School, the Head-of-School Office is the very first office one comes to upon entering the school's reception area. It is easily seen and accessible to students, parents, guests, and teachers. The office has windows looking out to the main school grass quad on one side and a window that looks into the office area itself.

Kids are able to pass by the office window on the quad side and wave hello or check their appearance in the window's reflection, a regular student practice. On the office side, the head of school can see every guest who enters the reception area. This allows the head of school to greet anyone and everyone who enters, as needed or desired. The office placement and windows alone express the school's strong culture of welcoming the guests (*hachnasat orchim*).

What's inside the office can be equally impressionable. When I was head of school, the first thing a guest saw when entering my office was a photo of every former student who served in the American or Israeli defense forces. They also saw hundreds of books, including a complete set of school yearbooks, a Jewish text section, and a lot of literature and philosophy. I displayed small American and Israeli flags in a de Toledo High School coffee mug, some certificates honoring the school, some Jewish art, and a large map of the world behind my desk. There were photos of my family and a not-so-organized array of files and documents on my working desk. There was also a signed baseball from Sandy Koufax, and a bulletproof vest hung over the back of my chair.

These cultural messages were intentional and abounding: We appreciate and honor those who serve in the defense of our lands. We are Zionistic. We care about deep learning. We love art. We like to brag about our school. We are part of a larger world to which we have a sacred responsibility. Family and community are important. The head of school is a Dodger fan of a certain era, he must juggle a lot of paper on his desk, and he is ready to protect the children in the school. Indeed, "everything matters, every time."

The Faculty Room: The Ideas "Trading Floor"

At de Toledo High School, staff is fortunate to have a single, large faculty work space that can accommodate a desk for every teacher in an open-architecture format. It also has private office spaces and a quiet lounge where teachers can make calls or just sit and think. Teachers sit by departments but have easy access to any faculty member in any department. In essence, the space itself cultivates the culture of community. It's also an effective way for teachers to exchange curricular ideas, brainstorm how to help struggling students, check in with new teachers, support one another intellectually and emotionally, and be motivated by the energy in the room. I would call it "the heartbeat" of school values and culture.

In designing such a space for your own school, the key is accessibility. Do teachers and administrators have access to each other? Can students easily find their teachers to ask a question or arrange a conference? Is the photocopy machine and coffee nearby? Does the space address teacher needs as indicated by the school's mission and promote a culture of collaboration and kindness?

Perhaps the best example of a "faculty room" is the original space at Bell Labs. The space embraced design visionaries, creative thinkers, computer engineers, electrical engineers, software designers, computer code writers, and business people all in one space. There, they had easy access to each other, and from there they fashioned and transformed the technological world we live in today.

The Principal's Office: Leadership from Within

At de Toledo High School, the Principal's Office is located at the south end of the faculty room. Her door is always open (unless she is in a meeting), and teachers never hesitate to walk in with questions, ideas, concerns, or need for guidance. The location of the office itself sends two important messages: First, the word *principal* is an adjective—she is the "principal teacher"; she is the lead educator and you can come to her for educational leadership. Second, she is there for you—all the time. The placement of the office and the work of the principal herself promote the culture of embrace by fostering community, collegiality, and unconditional support.

The College Guidance and Career Office: A Culture of Future Achievement

High school parents and students are often greatly concerned about post–high school prospects. As students and parents enter the lobby of de Toledo High School, one only has to turn right and walk twenty feet to enter the college guidance complex, where they will encounter three full-time college counselors, a receptionist, a work-and-research space, and a warm and inviting atmosphere. Again, the physical placement and actual work of the College Guidance and Career Office engenders a culture and symbolism that says the school cares deeply about the future, that we are here to guide you every step of the way, that there are hundreds of options depending upon the unique gifts of each child, and that all of this service is easily accessible.

Student Areas: Valuing Our Students

Physical spaces often make a statement about how the school values its students. Indeed, as our colleague Cheryl Finkel says, "School is about the kids," and let's never forget that. To this end, we should consider the beauty and efficacy of student lounges and hang-out areas, study and play areas, spaces for student meetings, locker placements and sizes, and the hallways in which students spend a portion of their day.

Of course, so much about physical spaces depends on the school's location, the local climate, resources, availability of space in and outside the building, and so forth. I will never forget the time I was giving a tour to a colleague from the northeastern part of the United States. He immediately noticed that many of the student lockers were relatively small and were located outside under an awning. He was confused. "What happens when it rains or snows, and where do the kids store their coats?" he asked. I chuckled a bit and explained that it never snows in Los Angeles, it rarely rains, and kids don't usually bring coats to school. Moreover, kids generally eat lunch outside on the grass quad—there is no indoor cafeteria space.

When visiting my colleague's school in the Northeast, I was eager to see their indoor cafeteria and other physical facilities and thereby observe how spaces might engender differences in culture. I was struck by the fact that the entire school was in one multistory building. The gym was part of the building, and the outdoor space was on the roof. Moreover, the cafeteria was in the basement and had no windows. At first I thought this was not good for kids. However, in my conversations with the students, they explained how they made their spaces work, how the space itself forced a certain kind of seriousness and focus on their studies, and frankly, they didn't know anything else so had no basis for comparison. Indeed, these students and their teachers had created a culture of strong academic focus and a beautiful comradery as they all sojourned in their close-knit space.

I tell these stories only to shed additional light on how physical spaces can shape a school's culture and ethos, how outdoor spaces versus indoor spaces might have an effect on the culture, and how educators must make best use of their physical spaces to ensure that the campus itself becomes part of the *who* of culture creation.

The Board Tour—Ron

At board consults, I take the members out to the street in front of the synagogue and tell them to pretend they were guests of the Bat/Bar Mitzvah from out of town who had never been there. Can you find the name of the place driving in from all directions? Can you see the address clearly from all directions? Any sign of welcome? What about parking space—are all the closest spaces saved for the rabbi, cantor, and board president? Are there dedicated spaces for visitors? Is it clear how and where to enter the building itself? Is there an automatic door option for guests in wheelchairs? Is there a mezuzah on the door that can be reached from a wheelchair, especially at the entrance to the sanctuary? Is there a wheelchair to borrow? Are there umbrellas to borrow? Plastic covers for wet umbrellas brought into the building? Once inside, can you find the rabbi's study? Restrooms? Coatroom? Is the coatroom tidy . . . or a dumping ground for junk? Is there comfortable seating in the lobby and gathering areas?

Of course, this story is applicable to schools or any institution that wants to promote a culture of welcome, community, embrace, and attention to even the smallest details to make those entering the space comfortable.

Swag: Wearing Culture on Our Sleeves

Swag is usually considered a vehicle for promoting the school's brand, for getting its name into the public eye, to gain good notoriety, and to create a sense of community and attachment to one's alma mater. Consider, however, if we also use swag to promote school culture, to impart the institution's values. In other words, swag becomes another inanimate *who* of school culture. What is the message we inscribe upon our spirit wear, pens, pads, bags, and anything else the school wants to give away? Have we thought carefully about that message? Have we considered the selection of words, graphic designs, fonts, colors, and materials?

Is the clothing practical, comfortable, and stylish? Will the students, teachers, parents, and board members be proud to wear it or purchase it for others? And, oh yes, have we considered where the clothing or other items are made? The polo shirts, T-shirts, sweatshirts, sweatpants, mufflers, hats, socks, jackets, pens, notebags, tote bags, banners, car decals, umbrellas, *tallitot*, donor awards, teacher awards, diplomas, faculty gifts for the holidays, and table gifts presented at the gala—are they made locally or overseas? Wherever they are produced, are the workers treated fairly?

Everything we do sends a message about a school's culture, how we do business, what we believe, and that of which we are most proud. These messages are mostly subtle and unspoken. Yet they are exceptionally loud.

Swag Goes to the Eiffel Tower—Bruce

One of our board members told me how, on a family trip to Paris, they were standing at the top of the Eiffel Tower. One of their sons, a student at the previously named New Community Jewish High School, was wearing a school T-shirt. Another American family was standing close by and walked over to our board member and her family. They exclaimed, "Your son goes to New Jew? We've heard so many wonderful things about that school. Is it true that the students are so kind? You must have an amazing culture there." As it turned out, the other family was Catholic. They had their children enrolled at one of our local Catholic schools. The student's "New Jew" T-shirt engendered a wonderful conversation between two American families, standing at the top of the Eiffel Tower, in Paris, France, seven thousand miles from their homes in Los Angeles.

Swag Goes to the Gym—Bruce

Twice a week I work out at one of our local gyms. Invariably I wear some kind of de Toledo clothing, usually a T-shirt and sweatpants, along with branded de Toledo socks. On the back of one of the T-shirts is the inscription "Be an A+ Human Being." While I was doing my usual light weights and stretches, a very large gentleman, covered with tattoos and rippling with muscles, asked me if he may have a word. I must admit I was a bit nervous. He took me aside and inquired about the words on the back of my shirt. I explained that de Toledo High School was a Jewish day school and the inscription was a one-sentence summation of one of our core goals. We then engaged in a wonderful conversation about the values of our nation, and he asked if I could explain more about Jewish ideas, beliefs, and values. I made a friend that day, the school became better known beyond the Jewish world, and another friend was made for the Jewish people—all because of school swag.

Questions for Crafting Your Culture

1. Who are the *who*s in your school? Who most powerfully embodies the culture?
2. How can these influencers be engaged to promote your school's culture?
3. What do people already do to promote school culture through language and actions, and how can they do more of it?
4. What roles do the students play in creating and promoting your school culture?
5. How can students become even more engaged in strengthening the culture?
6. How can the school or institution head and board become major players in creating, shaping, and executing your school's culture?
7. What is the impact of your school's culture on student learning and overall outcomes?

4

The *How* of Building and Sustaining School Culture

In the previous chapters, we developed an understanding of the *what* and the *who* of school culture—specifically the philosophy and the language of crafting a culture of academic excellence and AP kindness. In this chapter we offer suggestions for *how* to create that culture. Whereas much of the *how* is certainly interlaced within the previous chapters, and most educators will easily extrapolate the language, the *who*, and the *what* into their schools' processes, actions, and programs, this chapter will be more explicit, offering ideas and activities that may help your school community embed culture into every aspect of school life.

Please keep in mind that whereas most of the examples below are particular to high schools, I hope they demonstrate "best principles" and serve as templates for use at any level of schooling or, for that matter, in any kind of organizational structure.

Foundational Questions of *How*

In building school culture and values, ancient texts often offer foundational guideposts and questions as powerful reference points, which may become embedded in the school's language and behaviors.

My dear friend Gregg Alpert introduced me to a section of the Babylonian Talmud, *Masechet Shabbat* 31a, that speaks to such foundational questions. In this section of the Talmud, one of the rabbis describes six questions that God will ask of us when we pass from this world. In brief, they are:

1. Were you honest in business?
2. Did you make a set time to study?
3. Did you raise up community (children)?
4. Did you have hope?
5. Did you act with wisdom?
6. Did you understand a big thing from a small thing, and a small thing from a big thing?

At de Toledo High School, these questions, in an expanded form, became the expected schoolwide learning results (ESLRs) for every aspect of school life. These questions are posted in every classroom and in every office. Teachers often refer to them when making assignments, creating their disciplinary protocols, analyzing literature, or doing science experiments.

For example, when learning Shakespeare's *Macbeth*, an English teacher might ask, "How was the character of Macbeth not honest in his business?" Or, "Where can we find hopeful moments in the play?" Or, "Who acted with wisdom in the play? Who avoided wisdom, replacing it with ambition and greed?"

Another example might be while learning science. The teacher might integrate some of the six questions by asking, "How does science continue to advance? What kind of continuous study and experimentation must be done to make new discoveries?" Or, "What are the big ideas and concepts that keep pushing science forward, and what are those forces that detract from scientific progress?" And finally, the teacher might inquire, "How does science engender hope in our world? Can we gain wisdom from our scientific research?"

If we expand the culture-building lens, these six questions become the basis for achieving the school's ultimate educational goals for a student's lifetime, and they form the basis for overall school language. During times of crisis, such as the COVID-19 pandemic of 2020, students are reminded on a regular basis to have hope and find ways to engender hope within their families and communities. Doing community service projects, for instance, might help to answer the question "Did you have hope?" Moreover, in this case, the idea of hope offers a pathway for hopeful actions and a cultural shift away from despair, negativity, and hopelessness.

These questions even help to change the language and often the mindset of students when interacting with their teachers and parents. The question "Did you act with wisdom?" might encourage students to seek wisdom from their parents and teachers. It might engender questions about where we find wisdom, what wisdom looks like, how we know wisdom when we hear it, and how we adjust our lives to become receptacles of that wisdom.

In essence, these questions help to focus the entire school culture on what is, indeed, important in life. The questions remind students that within the daily rush to finish homework, or their angst about current news, or everyone's constant participation in social drama, perhaps everyone should take time to pause and reflect upon that which is unimportant and that which really matters over the short- and long-term journey of life.

Kodesh Moments

In the founding year of de Toledo High School, our school rabbi, David Vorspan, reasoned that whereas we had imparted to the students a strong set of values (as outlined in chapter 2), we seemed to be missing a practical pathway to the actualization of those values. What did it mean, for example, to be an "A+ human being"? How could a student (or board or faculty, for that matter) actualize the value of "circle of friends" or "not speaking *lashon hara*"?

To answer this question, Rabbi Vorspan introduced the concept and language of "*kodesh* moments." He explained to the students that *kodesh* might mean "holy," but it could also refer to a sense of apartness or specialness. *Kodesh* moments were construed as actions that pushed against the general ethos of the mundane, or the unimportant, or the cruelty that we often witness on a daily basis in the general society. (Remember, when this concept was introduced in September 2002, only a year had passed since the horrors of September 11, 2001. We were only a year from the subsequent firebombing of mosques, the regular destruction of Black churches, and even the villainization of the State of Israel as somehow involved in this epic American tragedy, to mention only a few of the painful moments at that time in history.)

In many ways, *kodesh* moments became an antidote, almost an elixir, to refocus our community on acts of *chesed* (kindness), *rachamim* (mercy), and *tzedakah* (justice).

Rabbi Vorspan explained that students, teachers, and board members could perform *kodesh* moments in many different ways. Such a moment could be as simple as inviting a fellow student to join you for lunch (circles of friends), or cleaning up your mess after lunch (*baal tashchit*, "do not waste"), or saying thank you to your teachers at the end of every class session. Or these moments might include running a blood drive, raising money for the homeless, or treating the security and maintenance staff with special kindness, respect, and dignity (every person is created in the "image of God").

For the teachers, imagine if they now regarded their work in the classroom, day in and day out, as *kodesh* moments or regarded the aha moments of the students as somehow holy. This kind of thinking helps to elevate teaching, every day, to a level of dignity and importance not often realized or acknowledged.

At the board level, imagine if these dedicated volunteers regarded every tuition assistance dollar awarded as a *kodesh* moment, or every board-level committee meeting as a *kodesh* moment because they are ensuring the sustainability of the school, or just showing up as a volunteer as a *kodesh* moment.

Welcoming New Parents and Students

Whether you are running a high school or a preschool, the process by which families and students are welcomed and oriented to your institution must be a seamless fabric of cultural immersion.

How parents are regarded from their first call to the admissions office, their first interaction with school security, and their greetings from office staff when they walk in the door are all vital to what the journalist Malcolm Gladwell calls the "blink" moment, wherein the school's culture is embedded in a person's mind.

As you establish your own school's protocols for welcoming, begin by placing yourself in the mind of the parents. What might be your own fears and concerns when entering a new situation? What would make you feel embraced? How best would your concerns and fears be alleviated?

For example, in the old TV show *Cheers*, one of the lines in the opening song says it all:

> *Sometimes you want to go*
> *where everybody knows your name*
> *And they're always glad you came.*[1]

In what follows, we offer some suggestions and examples of welcoming.

New Student Welcome

For new students to de Toledo High School, the welcoming begins at an open house for new students, usually occurring in November of the year before they enroll. We host a beautiful Sunday brunch for the five hundred people in attendance, followed by presentations in the gym by the arts department, the athletic department, the head of school, and student speakers.

At the end of the formal presentations, all of the prospective new students, mostly ninth graders, are escorted into a separate room where they are greeted by current students and the ninth-grade dean. In this thirty-five-minute session, with only one adult in the room, the students are free to ask questions and speak directly to students who may be just a year or two apart in age. Such a meeting sends a powerful message—we trust and value what you have to say; we regard you as "adults" able to moderate your own discussions and needs. It is the beginning of many cultural moments for the new students where they hear the "still small voice" that says, "The school regards each of you as unique and valued."

After the new student meeting and a separate Q&A for the adults, where they are able to ask questions of current and alumni students, the community reassembles and is then invited to visit classrooms, where teachers display their curriculum or run activities for the families.

Over the next several weeks, each family receives a personal phone call from the admissions office, dean, or even the head of school, checking in on their experience at the open house, inviting them for a school tour with a carefully selected buddy currently enrolled in grade nine, and ensuring that students and parents can easily fill out the online application. We also make sure they see the box to check that indicates if they need tuition assistance.

Additional check-in calls are made up until the week of admitting the students, usually in early March.

Post-Admission Welcome

Once students are admitted, several things happen. First, we provide the parents and students with a schedule for the upcoming school year, and we are careful to emphasize the dates for the ninth-grade retreat that occurs several days before the start of school. This allows parents to plan vacations around that date and be sure to have their ninth grader back in time for this all-important three-day, two-night retreat.

Second, parents are invited to the "Havdalah and Dessert" celebration for new parents. This event is held in June, usually before school lets out. It usually takes place at the home of a board member with a large enough backyard to accommodate about two hundred people. It begins after Shabbat is officially over, around 9 p.m. in Los Angeles at that time of year, to embrace all levels of Shabbat observance. Most teachers also attend this event, along with members of the Parent Organization.

The program is simple: a beautiful array of desserts, wine, coffee, and tea; and a great display of cheeses and fresh vegetables. Around 9:30 p.m., everyone is invited to create large circles around the Havdalah table set up in the middle of the yard. The music director sings a few songs of welcome, the head of school gives a five-minute talk about children's separation from middle school and the journey into high school, and then the school rabbi explains each of the rituals in the service and chants the ten-minute ceremony.

The entire event is over by 11 p.m. In those two hours, the parents gain a firsthand understanding of what we mean by community at the high school. They leave having made new friends and, in many cases, reconnecting with people they may have known during their children's elementary school years. Sometimes parents who haven't seen each other since high school or college will reconnect. The parent culture now begins to form.

Ninth-Grade Retreat

For de Toledo High School, the school year usually begins on a Thursday in late August. During the week before school starts, the entire ninth-grade class—along with their main teachers, dean, and principal—board busses and make their way to the Brandeis-Bardin Campus of American Jewish University, a three-thousand-acre retreat center about thirty minutes from the school, to experience forty-eight hours of bonding, learning the school's culture and traditions, and being oriented to the expectations and logistics of navigating their new high school.

This retreat is the beginning of a series of signature cultural moments for the students' journey through their next four years. Whereas they begin the retreat from over twenty different middle schools, they return after forty-eight hours together as a unified de Toledo High School community.

On the evening that the students arrive at the camp, the head of school gives a twenty-minute talk highlighting the five key goals of the school's culture of how to be an A+ human being. In brief, the students are introduced to the following concepts:

- Being an A+ human being is of equal or greater importance in life than being an A student.
- Everyone is enrolled in "Advanced Placement Kindness."

- No cliques, only circles of friends.
- Always avoid speaking *lashon hara* (evil speech or gossip).
- Strive for academic excellence.

(See chapter 1 for a complete explanation of these ideas.)

Each of these ideas is explained with examples and outcomes. Moreover, these five goals become guiding principles for the students and are repeated continuously at various times by teachers and administrators throughout the school year. They also become the foundational underpinnings of the school's approach to discipline and, of course, to the ultimate goals of a de Toledo High School education.

On the final morning of the retreat, all of the ninth-grade students gather in front of a sheer twelve-foot-high challenge wall. Their task is to ensure that every one of their classmates gets over the wall. (Strong faculty members stand on a landing on the back of the wall to reach over and assist as needed.) The students, without faculty help or verbal directions, must plan on how they intend to hoist one hundred students over the wall. It is a real test of organizational skills, values, planning, some brute strength, kindness to those who are fearful of the challenge, leadership, and community building.

At the end of the forty-five-minute exercise, every student has made it over the wall. (There are always some exceptions—a few students who prefer to sit out the challenge.) The ultimate result of this challenge is the unification of the class into a singular and powerful group with a sense that they can do anything if they act as an intelligent community and treat each other with respect and kindness. This exercise, in essence, cements the culture, values, and goals taught on the first evening of the retreat, and this learning continues to resonate over the next four years.

Opening Day

Like everything else within the cultural matrix of the high school, opening day at de Toledo High School is celebrated within a special set of rituals that often set the cultural tone for the school year.

Typically school begins around 8 a.m., but most of the students arrive early on the first day of school. Students mill about in the large lobby area giving the normal teenage hugs and shrieks indicating that "I haven't seen you all summer!"

Then, without warning, the seniors, who have secretly gathered in some spot near the parking garage, suddenly burst into the lobby with balloons and chants. Some students cheer the seniors, and every student looks forward to the moment when they get to do the same thing.

Everyone is then ushered into an opening assembly in the auditorium. Here student speakers and the head of school provide the theme for the year, and the board president provides a special greeting. Typical welcome-back announcements and directions are given, and then the music director leads the school in the alma mater song. (The ninth graders know the words, since they have just come back the day before from their ninth-grade orientation retreat.)

Students then adjourn to their first-period classes with administrators on guard to guide lost ninth graders and other new students toward their assigned classrooms.

The entire opening festivities, which take less than forty-five minutes, set a cultural tone of celebration for the new school year and provide the students with a sense of vision and fun. School can now begin. The culture of embrace is in place.

Signature School Trips

In addition to the normal grade-level retreats and bonding experiences, de Toledo High School offers three signature cultural moments for the students—two different tenth-grade trips to Israel and the eleventh-grade journey to the South to learn about the southern Jewish experience and the history of and struggle for civil rights in America.

By second semester of ninth grade, the students are abuzz, talking about the upcoming Israel experience. There are two choices: a two-week trip or a three-month residential sojourn. Both trips involve living in the homes of Israeli families, making permanent connections and lifetime friendships with those families, gaining a deep understanding of the culture and politics of the modern State of Israel, engendering a love and appreciation for the achievements of the Jewish state, and developing some modicum of independence and even grit while living nine thousand miles away from home and school. These experiences are truly Israel education, a full immersion into the what was, what is, and what can be for the Jewish people.

Upon the student's return from their time in Israel, the cultural impact on the students and the school is profound. Students grasp in an almost "DNA" sort of way that the Jewish people are united and inseparable and that the American and Israeli Jewish communities must stand together in mutual support. Israel is no longer a news story in the local press; rather, it is a living, breathing, very complex society, and it is the most important seminal Jewish triumph since the destruction of the Second Temple in 70 CE. Returning students take leadership roles in Israel support activities on campus; some enter into the wider community, joining the myriad of Israel support organizations of all political persuasions; and all bring back to the school a greater maturity and perspective. They begin to understand more deeply a "big thing from a small thing."

In fall of the eleventh grade, usually November, the juniors travel to Atlanta, Georgia, for their one-week southern Jewish experience and civil rights tour. Their journey begins in Atlanta, where they board a bus and make overnight stops along the way, ending up in Memphis, Tennessee. On their journey they meet historic figures of the civil rights movement. They meet southern Jews who have their own special narrative of our nation's history and struggles, and most importantly, they greatly expand their vision of what and who America is while also exploring the Jewish and American values and culture that make up this great experiment in democracy and liberty. Upon returning home, students are once again transformed—more mature and more nuanced in their ability to enhance the culture of their school and their communities.

All-School Shabbaton

As described in chapter 3, perhaps the most effective signature moment in developing de Toledo High School's culture is the all-school Shabbaton. This event entails all four hundred students and one hundred faculty and staff residing together at a local camp for four days and three nights. Usually hosted during the spring in California, when the weather is generally warm (of course, the weather is always good in Southern California, except when it's not), most of the event's programs take place under the canopy of a beautiful natural setting.

Students and faculty work together for several months planning the program for this gathering, thereby achieving great buy-in on everyone's part. As spring approaches, the excitement and desire to attend are palpable. (The cost of the Shabbaton is a part of the school fees, and all permission slips are signed upon registering for school, so no extra burdens are placed upon students or parents.)

It should also be noted that whereas attending the Shabbaton is part of teacher contracts, they are not required to stay overnight at the camp (which is located a reasonable distance from everyone's homes in Los Angeles). Yet, since the faculty understands the importance of this event to the school's culture, almost all of our teachers, and often their spouses and families, are eager to remain at camp for all three nights.

What is even more remarkable is that alumni, after at least one year of college or other post–high school experience, are invited to become counselors at the Shabbaton. They not only cannot wait to return and give back to their school, but they also embody the school's culture of kindness and embrace for the current students. There can be no more powerful statement for our kids than seeing the "elders" live and promote the school's culture and values.

So now what happens?

The formal programs at the Shabbaton reflect the school's educational goals, which are achieved in a relaxed and informal setting. More importantly, however, for the purposes of our cultural goals, the informal programs—or what we like to call the "liminal spaces"—are where all of the school's values and culture of embrace take flower. It is the informal moments—for example, conversing with teachers while walking to the next program—where students learn to appreciate these adults as role models and as completely dedicated to their education. Just "showing up" for the Shabbaton is a powerful message sent by teachers to their students.

It is in the liminal spaces that students interact with each other, actualizing the values of "circles of friends" where no one is left out or avoiding negative language. Most importantly, in the liminal spaces, students recognize the unique gifts of each classmate, find new friends with whom to grow, and practice the actions of kindness that are so much a part of the school's culture.

Whereas the Shabbaton programs on Thursday and Friday are rich with content and learning, there are two ritual moments, both occurring on Shabbat, that synthesize the culture built over the previous school year.

First is the celebration of Shabbat on Friday night. Imagine a dining hall filled with five hundred students, faculty, staff, and guests, sharing a beautiful meal together. As part of the Friday night ritual, parents usually bless their children at the dinner table. In the absence of parents, the students and teachers bless each other. For some it is a moment of embrace and tears. At the end of the meal, everyone moves their chairs into multiple rows of a semicircle (yes, it's noisy) for thirty minutes or more of community singing led by the charismatic music director.

After singing, each grade breaks into special program spaces for some kind of unique bonding experience. The seniors adjourn to a large communal space, sit on the floor, and spend the next three hours expressing to one another their appreciation for being together over the past four years. It is a cultural touchpoint where something wonderful is said, unscripted, about every single senior. No one is left out of this circle of friends.

Grades nine, ten, and eleven each has its own specialized program of varying degrees of depth and seriousness. For example, the ninth graders might do a "speed-dating" program, while the tenth and eleventh graders may participate in programs that delve into spiritual and moral concerns of teens.

The second moment, and perhaps the most powerful, occurs at Havdalah on Saturday night. Just before Shabbat is over, the entire student and
faculty community gather at a large campfire amphitheater area (board
members are also present). Two seniors each give their *drishat shalom*
(senior sermon) to the entire school (usually about eight hundred words
each), followed by a keynote talk from the head of school. Announcements
are made and everyone then makes their way to the dining hall for dinner.

At the end of dinner, specific instructions are provided as to how we
exit the dining hall. It is now dark, and the community must make its way
to the Havdalah Garden, where each class will stand in one of the concentric circles around the Havdalah table set in the middle.

The top senior staff exit first so as to position themselves in the center
of the circles and stand around the Havdalah table, waiting for the students to arrive.

The twelfth graders then exit the dining hall and, upon arrival at the
garden, are each given a single long candle. They then form the inner circle closest to the Havdalah table.

Next, the eleventh graders exit, and upon arrival at the garden, they
too are given a single candle. They then form a circle around the seniors.

It should be noted that this choreography includes the music director
singing songs on a microphone inside the circles as the students arrive.

The tenth graders, followed by the ninth graders, soon arrive and form
two more circles around the seniors and juniors. The faculty and board
members form the outermost circle.

Students are asked to put their arms around each other for the dura-
tion of the Havdalah service.

Once everyone is in place, the senior staff member reads a specially
written, very short script that ends with part of Robert Frost's poem "Two
Roads." The school rabbi then explains the symbolism of each part of the
Havdalah service. At this point, the already-lit Havdalah candle is used
to light the single candles held by the senior staff. They turn around and
light the single candles of the seniors, who in turn light the candles of the
juniors (passing the torch both materially and symbolically). The seniors
and juniors then form groups of three or four students, holding the wicks

of their candles together to form the traditional four-wick Havdalah candle used for the ceremony. The music director then chants the very short service.

It is the holding of the candles—the symbolic passing of the torch, the realization by the seniors that they are almost finished with their high school journeys, and the realization by the juniors that they are now the school leaders—that crystallizes the ultimate cultural moment at the school by linking together the generations and cementing the notion of community. (A special thank you to Rabbi Uri Allen, who created the script and choreography of our Havdalah program.)

Needless to say, the tears of the seniors and juniors—boys and girls—abound, and when the seniors are asked to blow out their candles, they refuse, not wanting to let go of their special moment. Indeed, it takes the staff perhaps an additional twenty minutes to convince the seniors to leave the garden and move over to the campfire area, where the students then present maybe two dozen musical or whimsical acts of various kinds.

Saturday night at the Shabbaton is, in so many ways, the ultimate cultural synthesis; it is tangible; the emotions are real; and the memories are forever.

Drishot Shalom—Greetings of Peace

Each week at de Toledo High School, at the all-school assembly, seniors are asked to deliver what are called *drishot shalom*, or "greetings of peace." These eight-hundred-word talks, loosely based on some portion of the Bible (*Tanakh*) selected by the students and their mentors, are opportunities for seniors to impart their wisdom to the entire school community. Family members are invited to attend. It is a moment for the seniors to shine, for the underclass students to sit in awe of what they are hearing, and for every ninth grader to imagine him- or herself standing before the school four years later delivering their own talks.

Most importantly for the school, it is another cultural touchpoint. The students usually begin working on their talks in eleventh grade. Each student selects a mentor to guide them through the process. The mentors meet with the students on a regular basis to bat around ideas, examine first drafts, provide guidance on length and depth of the talks, and ensure that the students truly express what they hope to impart to their fellow students.

A staff member is assigned to coordinate the scheduling of the talks (up to one hundred each year), inviting the guests, and ensuring that whatever technology the students need is in place and working. The *drishat shalom* coordinator requires that the talks be submitted well before the scheduled dates of delivery to the school to check for accuracy and appropriateness within the context of our school's values. It should be noted here that by senior year the students are so immersed in the school's culture that a talk has never been rejected due to inappropriateness.

Perhaps the most moving and culturally powerful moment of each *drishat shalom* comes at the end of the talk (sometimes at the beginning), where the students offer their thank-yous. Of course, we always hear the expected appreciation for parents, teachers, and close friends. Sometimes there are surprise thank-yous for unexpected mentors of whom even the parents were unaware.

However, what is most stunning is *how* the students thank those who have guided them through their journeys up until the present moment. It is a moment of public vulnerability. They usually thank their parents last, and that appreciation comes with choked-up voices, tears, unabashed love and appreciation, and invariably huge hugs. It is a moment when the school's culture allows seventeen- and eighteen-year-olds, raised in the larger American society that often frowns on public displays of emotion—especially for boys—to show unbridled emotion in a safe space. No one is fearful that students will poke fun at them or think them "uncool" for openly loving and appreciating their parents. On the contrary, what has become "cool" is embrace and embracing, public support and supporting, kind words and kind action—indeed, the culture demands "advanced placement coolness."

Graduation

Most graduation ceremonies are for the enjoyment of parents and grandparents. While some schools fill that moment with many meaningful rituals, others rely on the proven formula of processional, speeches, perhaps a video of the graduates, and finally the handing out of diplomas.

What schools might consider is that the graduation ceremony itself is a cultural touchpoint for not only the students and their families but also for the entire community. It is a time to embed unique cultural rituals into the ceremony that are meaningful for the participants and send a powerful message to the larger community about who they are and what they value.

At de Toledo High School, the graduation ceremony opens with a brief statement from the principal about how the graduation honors not only the students but also the parents. Added to this message is how our ceremony is also a tribute to the teachers, to anyone who serves the community, and to those who served in the armed forces of America and Israel. The statement includes a tribute to Holocaust survivors who can now witness in the faces of the children the meaning and purpose of their survival. The introduction goes something like this.

I'd like to welcome you to an exciting moment in Jewish educational history—the fourteenth graduation ceremony of de Toledo High School.

Our graduation tonight is rich with meaning:

For our parents, grandparents, and great-grandparents, it means your legacy is secure.

For survivors of the Shoah who are among us tonight, it means Judaism is alive and vibrant.

For those who have served to protect America and Israel, we honor you.

Seventy-two years after the creation of modern Israel, it means that America stands with you.

And for our community, and the teachers who educate our children, it means a future of great leadership.

Thank you, and now, let us begin.

This statement sets the tone and explains that the graduation about to transpire holds an integrated vision of what our graduates mean to the community, to history, and to the world. It also sets up a vision for the graduates regarding their obligations to their community and to history.

The graduation continues with the typical script of the national anthem, a prayer from the rabbi, and four student speakers. The speakers, however, do not include the valedictorian and salutatorian. The school gives no awards at graduation. (Awards usually make the students not receiving them feel awful and in some ways is an embarrassment for families.)

Rather, the student speakers are selected by their peers without regard to grade-point average, participation in sports or extracurricular activities, or other standard measures of success. At de Toledo High School, the real measure of student success—the culture of success, if you will—is the high regard of their classmates. This is a powerful cultural statement about the values of the school. Without fail, the students select their peers who have performed the most community service hours, who have been the most kind over the last four years, who have been the most loyal friends, and who rarely, if ever, leave anyone out of their circle of friends.

At the end of the ceremony, the faculty adds one last piece to this moment already rich with meaning and symbolism. Once the head of school announces the traditional statement about "the power invested in me by our board of directors and the State of California, I now pronounce you officially graduated," the teachers immediately line up on both sides of the recessional aisle. Graduates then exit the stage through the line of teachers, who now surround the newly graduated seniors on both sides. Invariably the graduates are high-fiving their teachers and more often than not giving their teachers big hugs. There are tears, warm embraces, and whispered words of thanks by both teachers and students. (We make sure the aisle is wide enough to accommodate this moment.)

Symbolically, the teachers are "sending off" their former charges, and the students are walking through the symbolic "aisle of knowledge and values" that has been imparted to them over four years in high school.

Parents and guests watch this scene with awe and wonder. It is clear to all that the teachers and students formed a lifetime bond. It is also the final *kodesh* moment in their lives as high school students until they return as alumni, speakers, Shabbaton counselors, and eventually parents and board members.

The Aisles Have It—Ron

There is great power in aisles. In Australia, the bride and groom walk down the aisle to the ceremonial chuppah and as newlyweds they leave the party through two lines of family and guests. At the gravesite in Jewish tradition, the friends who come to support the family create an "aisle of comfort" through which mourners leave the graveside. In Congress, a high compliment is a representative who can work with colleagues "across the aisle."

Enculturation—Ron

The famous sociologist Margaret Mead termed the transmission of a culture from one generation to another "enculturation."[2] How does this happen? How do students, faculty, staff, and parents learn the norms—the standards of conduct of a culture? There are three ways:

1. Communication: you are told what the "rules" are for behavior in this culture.
2. Observation: you can watch what others do and how they act in the culture.
3. Participation: you jump into the culture and actively learn by doing.

While all three methods are in play at de Toledo High School, the central strategy is the active participation in the life of the school.

As their teacher, I witnessed this process unfold as the Vov class kids at B'nai Amoona in St. Louis continued their classroom community the following year by preparing for a unique living experience in Israel during the summer. Having developed their own normative classroom community, these kids from an American suburb were thrown into the culture of an Orthodox *moshav shitufi* (cooperative agricultural settlement), living for nine weeks with an Israeli family. To be accepted as something more than tourists, the students had to learn the norms of this different culture, moving from aspiring nonmembers—guests, if you will—to fully recognized (albeit temporary) members of the Israeli community. They did this by not only learning the norms through communication, observation, and participation but also by complying with the norms during their initial introduction into the community, just as the de Toledo students do during their first weeks in the school. As the American students became familiar with the norms of behavior, they began to identify with the community, counting themselves as members. Similarly, at de Toledo, the students adopt the school as their own, often wearing "swag," the branded clothing with the school logo and name.

By the end of the summer in Israel, the American students had earned their place in the community of the *moshav*, forming lifelong relationships with their host families. For students of de Toledo, their friendships with their peers and teachers become a lasting, integral part of their identities. The various rituals to welcome incoming students and to celebrate graduating students at de Toledo solidify this process.

Creating the Structure for Students

Like adults, students have a wide variety of personalities—confident, shy, aloof, disgruntled, and some just passing through. What all of these personality types need, however, is encouragement and a pathway for empowerment.

One simple tactic at de Toledo High School is the open-door policy on the part of the head of school. "Open door" simply means that any student may schedule time with the top administrators by asking the office staff to set up a meeting. As part of the policy, that meeting should occur within forty-eight hours of the request (better if the same day), not in the next two weeks. Students seeking meetings are usually excited about an idea or concern they wish to promote and a two-week wait for a teenager may feel like an eternity. By scheduling the meeting in short order, we send a message of tangible encouragement and validation that the "door" is truly open to students. (Of course, the guidelines for these meetings is to pitch new ideas and make suggestions for school change or improvement. They are not a time to, say, complain about a course or teacher. That meeting should be with the department chair, class dean, or principal. Ensuring that students know the protocols is part of school culture.)

Shy students may not understand what an open-door policy is or even feel confident enough to attempt to use it. A different pathway is in order for these students, which can be developed in various ways—a few of which are mentioned below.

- Small, ten-student mentor groups are created, led by a senior along with a faculty sponsor.
- Students are invited to pitch ideas for new clubs to a teacher or the grade-level dean.
- The head of school or principal proactively approaches students at lunch and asks if they have any suggestions to improve our school.

Another way to enhance the open door is to hold regular all-school town meetings. These meetings have two rules: (1) no complaining or gossip; and (2) if you propose a school challenge, you must also suggest a solution. Then the floor is open for anyone to speak. These meetings usually need forty minutes or so to be effective, depending, of course, on the school size. The head of school should lead the meeting, to provide an air of seriousness and project the message that all student ideas go directly to the "top." The students must also be aware that the head of school may rule things out of order or redirect a suggestion to another venue or member of the faculty team. It is recommended that the head of school log all ideas, perhaps writing them on a computer that projects the list to the entire room, without making positive or negative comments. At the next town meeting, the head of school can then report on progress on some of the ideas and explain that other ideas have been put on hold or rejected due to lack of viability. Kids can handle rejection; it's a good skill to have.

Student Discipline: The "Chuppah" Approach

Everything a school does should be based on its unique values and culture. Student discipline is an area where these values and the school's culture become vitally important.

I call how de Toledo High School views student discipline the "chuppah approach." A chuppah is the canopy under which a Jewish couple marries. It is the symbolic equivalent of the new couple's home, their private space, but it is also open on all sides. The chuppah allows for separation from and participation in the community.

Having been in education for five decades, I have had the opportunity to stand under or witness many chuppahs of former students. The experience of the chuppah has provided me with a long view of a child's life, and it reminds me that we must treat all human beings as if they were created in the image of God.

And here I use the metaphor of the chuppah as a reminder that kids grow up, they do indeed become adults, and how we treat them in school—the discipline we apply and the kindnesses we bestow—will be remembered by our students as they move toward the chuppah of their chosen professions, businesses, trades, arts, military service, and life partnerships.

So, now what happens if a child cheats on a test, disrupts a class, bullies another student, or commits some other violation of the school's rules? How does the chuppah approach work in the real world? How do the school's culture of embrace and values guide and even dictate how discipline is applied?

Whereas I cannot provide a guide for every disciplinary eventuality, below are a few examples that drive home the concept.

Kathi Edwards, de Toledo High School's first dean of students and the pioneer of our school's approach to discipline, was the "address" when teachers needed help in setting a student on the right path. Take, for example, cheating on a test. The first question Kathi would ask the cheating student is "Which of the school's values did you fail to live up to by cheating on the test?" By always remembering the chuppah approach—meaning that she hoped one day to meet this child as an adult under the chuppah of their lives—Kathi would engage the student in a conversation about the school's values and how the student might better live up to those values, and even how the student might strengthen the overall culture of honesty in the school.

She would then assign a consequence (not punishment) that made sense for the student within the context of the school's values and culture. (It should be noted that in addition to the consequences developed by the dean, the teacher still had the power to fail the child on the exam and average that grade into his or her overall grade average in the class.) Remember, Kathi's role was to engender in the student a moral compass for use over a lifetime. Her task was to figure out how to achieve that goal given the unique soul of each student. (And she would also confer with the teacher to gain greater insight into the student's needs.)

Perhaps a more poignant and complex example was the time a tenth-grade student was found with some illegal substances at our all-school Shabbaton—an expellable offense. Again, the dean met with the student and asked how he had violated the values and culture of the school. In this case, of course, we involved the parents, some teachers, and the head of school. The boy understood that he had harmed the community at large, that he had broken some laws, and that the consequences for his behavior would be quite severe.

Once again, the professional team overseeing the situation asked ourselves the "chuppah" question: How can we assure that this boy becomes the man we know he could be, that we not break his soul or spirit, and that we leave him with the understanding that one day we all hope to stand with him under the "chuppah" of his life? Of course, we also needed to make a clear statement to the school community that such violations could not in any way be embraced.

We decided to have the boy leave the community for one full year, with the stipulation that he could return to us in the twelfth grade. During his absence, and if he wanted to return to the community, he had to build a case for himself that his actions constituted enough evidence to allow him to return. The boy was distraught, and he even cried in my office, pleading that he be allowed to remain in school. However, he understood that he must leave. He also understood that the school held no rancor toward him and that if he could overcome his challenges, he would be welcomed "home" without prejudice.

He re-enrolled in twelfth grade and graduated in good standing. After high school, he went on to volunteer in the Israeli Defense Forces, and today we all stand with him proudly under the "chuppah" of his life.

The "chuppah" approach to discipline is simply one of perspective: applying wisdom to imagine children's lives beyond the school years and always avoiding the notion that children's actions as teens, or younger, somehow make them terminally "bad" people. To quote Mr. Miyagi from the movie *The Karate Kid*, "There are no bad students, only bad teachers." I believe that our teachers are not only good but great. Now let's ensure that our students know we will be under the "chuppah" with them throughout their lives.

Redundancy Is the Key to Communication

I have had the good fortune to travel widely throughout the world, and I know many friends and family who have done the same. What continually amazes me about these travels, aside from the obvious joy of seeing great sights, learning new cultures, and meeting new people, is the fact that no matter how remote my location, I can always get a Diet Coke. Indeed, I have been to places where I did not speak one word of the native tongue (I can get by in perhaps two or three languages) and the locals could not speak any language I knew, yet when I said "Diet Coke," the red and silver can of Coke magically appeared.

Perhaps the best example of this was when traveling in the Sinai desert. Our bus stopped at an intersection of a highway where there was nothing but flat desert for fifty miles in all directions. There were no phone or electric lines to be found. At the intersection, there was a black

Bedouin tent pitched by the side of the road selling drinks. The tent's owner spoke only one dialect of Arabic. Yet when I asked for a Diet Coke, the red and silver can appeared—ice-cold, I might add.

So, how is it possible that everyone in the world who sells soft drinks knows about Coca-Cola? I discovered the answer with a quick Google search. The Coca-Cola Company spends $4 billion worldwide each year on advertising. They understand that redundancy—never-ending repetition—is the key to communication about their product.

Needless to say, our schools and institutions do not have $4 billion a year to spend on advertising; most of us don't even have $40,000 to spend. Yet what we do have is a clearly defined, relatively small community within which we can repeat our message and our culture on a regular—even hourly—basis.

To achieve de Toledo High School's version of $4 billion worth of advertising, every adult in the school must be educated in the culture, language, symbols, and traditions of the place. More so, each adult—teacher, administrator, office worker, security guard, maintenance worker, parents, and board members—should "own" the language of the culture and use it at every opportunity—all the time, in every venue, in every space, to every student.

In the Classroom

Of course, the most obvious space, and the place where most student contact is accomplished, is in the classroom. In addition to posting written versions of the school's mission statement and ESLRs (expected schoolwide learning results) in the classroom, teachers should learn to intertwine their lessons with the school's cultural vernacular.

I remember taking a statistics class as a requirement for my doctoral studies at the University of Southern California (USC). Every day, the professor would enter the lecture hall and greet us with "Good morning, Trojans." (The Trojan was the school's mascot.) I thought it was pretty silly at the time—after all, we were graduate students studying for doctorates. Yet in that "silliness" was a powerful and redundantly communicated message—we were part of the Trojan family; we were a team, cheerleaders for the USC brand, and we ought to be loyal to our tribe. In essence, he instilled some USC values at every class meeting.

Now imagine a teacher walking into her third-grade class and asking the students, "Who can tell me if they did a good deed yesterday?" or "Before we start our math lesson, who can describe how they might have been honest in their interactions with a classmate?" Perhaps at the end of the math lesson the teacher says, "I have such hope for this entire class since I saw so much excellence today in our study of math."

In this scenario, the teacher integrates the school's cultural language into her regular speech and continues to do so throughout the day, the week, and the year. Perhaps by the time the second semester rolls around, the students might even begin to use the cultural reference points of good deeds, honesty, and hope in their own conversations with parents and friends.

Changing Faculty Culture to Match the Values—Bruce

Betty Winn was head of Heschel Day School in Northridge, California, for ten years. She was only the second head of school, following the beloved founder, Shirley Levine. Betty wanted to ensure that the school's value of lifelong learning was a lived reality. Here is her story.

When I started at Heschel, a core value was lifelong learning. It was written in the mission statement that students would develop as lifelong learners. Yet when I brought a consultant into the school through a Partnership for Excellence in Jewish Education (PEJE) Improvement Journey Grant, the consultant did not witness a culture of lifelong learning among the faculty and staff. When he spent time with them, they did not talk about professional development or a commitment to ongoing learning in their craft and personal lives, but rather they spent their time talking in the faculty room about everything and anything not related to creating a growth mindset.

When he brought this to my attention, my eyes were opened. A school is a place of learning. If our faculty was not committed to our core value of lifelong learning, and they were not serving as role models in that way, how did we expect our students to value their learning and become lifelong learners? As a result, I conducted meetings with our administration, faculty, and staff to develop a plan to support teachers and provide opportunities for their professional growth as well as for collective programs and collaboration. The division leaders met with their teams as well as individual teachers to set goals for moving forward and supporting their efforts to meet those goals. As the head of school, I also met with the board and shared the need for aligning a core value and our culture. We developed new programs into our strategic plan and provided necessary financial resources to ensure the goals would be met.

As a result, within two years the culture changed completely with respect to lifelong learning and professional development. Ultimately not only did the teachers find greater satisfaction in their work but the students benefited from the learning of their teachers.

Kol ha-Kavod (With All Honor)—Ron

Early in my career at American Jewish University, I received a phone call from Metuka Benjamin, the powerhouse head of all schools at Stephen Wise Temple, a huge Reform synagogue that shared our mountaintop in Los Angeles on Mulholland Drive. She was planning an all-day faculty retreat and had heard me lecture about "creating community in the classroom." Metuka was inviting me to speak to her large one hundred-plus faculty about that very topic. But she wanted to meet in advance to discuss some "values" issues that had cropped up in the school.

At our meeting, Metuka explained that there were several challenges in the day school: (1) the Americans and the Israelis were often at odds, like the Hatfields and the McCoys; (2) the general studies and Hebrew language teachers were often at odds, like the Hatfields and the McCoys; and (3) the nonsmokers and the smokers (in those days, there were still plenty) were often at odds, like the Hatfields and the McCoys. "Your job, Ron, is to teach them how to build a community among themselves!"

The Stephen Wise campus was in a construction phase, so I began by using "building" as my metaphor for the talk. "I'm used to wearing a kippah when entering a synagogue or school. Let me show you the one I chose for today"—and then I pulled out a white hard hat, the kind construction crews wear, and put it on my head. The mostly female teachers howled with laughter, and it got their attention. I talked of the "building blocks of community"—that is, creating interpersonal relationships by getting to know each other personally through sharing one another's stories; by collaborating together on projects such as devising "integrated" curricula of Jewish and general subjects; by respecting one another's space; and by celebrating one another's achievements.

Most importantly, I spoke of the values that ought to infuse the faculty room culture: every human being is shaped to be a *b'tzelem Elohim*, a reflection of God, and a practitioner of Godliness. Then I got blunt: "No *lashon hara*; no stealing of someone else's bulletin board ideas without permission; and no smoking in the faculty lounge—it bothers the nonsmokers. So please go outside if you must light up. Remember, each of you is doing the sacred work of teaching our children. You—each of you—is one of God's angels on earth. You are *malachei ha-shareit*, the 'angels who serve.' Treat one another like angels . . . and your school will soar to the heavens and beyond!"

The teachers were stunned that I had done my homework to learn what the pressure points were and that I was willing to be blunt and direct. I was a young professor talking to a bunch of veteran teachers and, frankly, I thought I was likely to be booed out of the room. Instead, the room exploded in a standing ovation. Metuka wore a smile from ear to ear. She called me a week later to report that the culture in the faculty room had changed for the better, literally overnight.

In the Boardroom

Ideally, your school's culture also resonates with the board. I remember being at a board meeting where there was some kind of contentious discussion on the table about raising next year's school tuition even though the school had run a small budget surplus in the current year. Did we really need to raise the tuition? The board had a decision to make that would affect every family in the school. In the midst of the often heated yet respectful dialogue, the board chair reminded the board members about one of our core values by asking, "What would it look like for us to be completely honest in business as we decide on the tuition increase?" There was a reflective silence in the room, and in that one moment of cultural reminder, of remembering how their actions would affect the perception of parents and community regarding how the school conducts its business, the conversation came to consensus and the tuition was set at the lower amount.

In another example, de Toledo High School had just purchased its new campus and had about a year to complete the renovations so that students could occupy the facilities the following year. The original plan was to spend $20 million on the renovation. The development committee and the development professionals began their work to raise the money. After about three months of an aggressive campaign, questions arose whether or not we could raise the full $20 million in time. Would we need to incur bank debt to complete the project? Once again, the school's culture and values came to the rescue. One of the board members asked one of the six questions found in the school's expected schoolwide learning results: "Are we acting with wisdom? Is it wise to saddle the school with debt? Wouldn't the payments on that debt diminish the funds we could spend on the kids' education? And, of course, are we being honest in our core business, which is not construction but education?"

Again, cultural reminders had the desired effect. The facilities chair called the architect and builder and told them to figure out a way to do $10 million worth of renovations and we would shelve the remaining plans for a later date. The $10 million was raised, the school incurred no construction debt, and to this day the school remains debt-free. The practical impact of the culture ultimately led to a far more robust core product—higher-quality education for our children.

In the Gym, on the Sports Field, in the Arts Programs

Most educators would agree that perhaps one of the most important and powerful venues for building school culture of kindness and embrace is in a school's extracurricular activities, especially sports and the arts. Here the coaches and specialists exercise enormous cultural power. Since students usually choose to take a sport or specialize in the arts, their commitment to those choices creates deep engagement and a certain loyalty to the adult in charge. In essence, the students give a priori permission to the coaches and teachers to guide their charges as they see fit. This fact provides an opportunity for even deeper cultural understanding and action.

For example, most schools aspire to ban negative speech—namely, gossip, hurtful Facebook posts, verbal bullying, and so forth. Imagine the basketball coaches, for instance, explicitly banning negative or hurtful speech during practice or at games. Imagine the non-Jewish coach saying to her Jewish players, "We do not speak *lashon hara* on our team, ever. If I hear it, you will be benched. And if it continues, you can no longer be a member of our school's team." I've seen this in action, and once students overcome their surprise at hearing Hebrew from their coach, they understand that the culture of positive speech at the school is no joke and they, with few exceptions, fully comply.

In other cultural moments, coaches teach their students that advanced placement kindness is more important than winning games. The coaches encourage players to always lend a helping hand to members of the opposing team if they should fall down or get injured.

So, too, in the theater arts program. At de Toledo High School, a day before opening night, the show's lead came down with the flu. She was a senior and this was to be the shining moment of her school career on stage. Her disappointment was overwhelming. At the end of the eight-day run of the show, at the final performance, the ill student felt healthy enough to attend, sitting in the audience. At the moment of final bows, and without the knowledge of the director, the students went down into the audience and escorted their castmate onto the stage. The audience exploded in applause. The director, after all, had engendered advanced placement kindness among her actors during every rehearsal. The students understood their obligation to act upon this value within the context of the school's culture.

At Lunchtime

At most schools, and at every grade level, lunch hour is an ideal time to build and to cement a school's culture of embrace and kindness. It is also a time to evaluate whether or not the school's culture and values are working. Typically, in most schools, there are several teacher supervisors in the lunchroom or on the yard, mainly for safety reasons. In general, however, students are on their own to sit where and with whom they want. Most are out of the direct supervision of the faculty and are free to behave as they will. This is the moment to do a check on the culture.

Throughout the days of school at de Toledo High School, students are reminded that the school's culture of advanced placement kindness, circles of friends, and no negative speech—to name a few of the prevailing values—is not just for the classroom or when adults are present. Rather, the cultural ideals are expected to be lived all the time, even if no one is watching.

As the head of the school, I would often wander around the areas where students congregated for lunch. (Being at a Southern California school, most of the kids ate outside on the lawn or at tables.) I would not hesitate to surprise a group of ninth-grade students, sit down with them, and engage in a conversation about school culture. The conversation would often begin by asking the ninth graders, "Who are you?" Invariably I would get the teenage eye-roll and then hear their rehearsed response: "Dr. Powell, we are a circle of friends, not a clique. You are welcome to join us at our table anytime." (Of course, this response had been taught to them at their recent ninth-grade retreat.)

They knew, of course, that that was the response I wanted. What they did not know is that I was encouraging them to be redundant about the school's values and culture. And whereas we all could have a good laugh at my expense, their response allowed me to open up a deeper conversation about how we can all do better at "welcoming the stranger" and what this means for the larger society in America. Can we, indeed, form a circle of friends with the Black and Latino communities, with LGBTQ communities, and with those communities without homes? What would that circle look like? What kind of power might emanate from such circles?

By the time these students were in tenth grade, and certainly by eleventh grade, when I walked up to a lunch table, I never needed to ask the question "Who are you?" I was immediately invited to join them for lunch, and they would initiate the conversation about how our school might do better in building community.

A Final Word on Redundancy

Needless to say, repeating the language that embraces the culture of a school is vital in sustaining and increasing its effect. I could go on and on providing examples and venues for that repetition. Suffice it to say that whether at school retreats, in the hallways, in the parking lot, or at school dances, teachers and hopefully the older students continue to find opportunities to embrace and act upon the school's culture. The goal is to talk the culture, demonstrate the culture, and invite others to participate in and increase the depth of that culture.

Changing Culture

I understand that you may be a head of school that may have a less-than-stellar culture or even a negative or toxic cultural environment. The challenge is how to change it. How do you move from the negative to the positive? While the focus of this book is not change management, I will offer some brief ideas in this section that may help you get started in the change process.

First, know what you want to change and be sure others believe that change is needed. Max Weber, the great sociologist and philosopher, believed that all change moves from the bottom to the top. To begin changing a culture, I suggest starting with the teachers, the office staff, the parents, and the students. Ask their opinions; structure and hold small-group meetings that allow people to voice their feelings about the current culture. Ask these constituents for ideas about how they suggest changing their school for the better. Listen carefully, writing down their ideas and thoughts, and keep people informed about any changes you may consider proposing. Once the data is collected, publish it. Be transparent. Before making any real change, vet it first with the constituents. Bring people into the process.

If a goal for cultural change, for example, is greater buy-in and transparency among the professional staff on all or many of school operations or educational policies, I suggest structuring and creating regular agenda-driven meetings within the school—weekly for the administrative staff, weekly for department chairs or division principals, weekly for teachers at each grade level, weekly for the office staff, and weekly for any other group you deem vital for cultural change. Hold all-faculty meetings every three weeks or so, and be sure to begin those meetings with "shout-outs." For our purpose, shout-outs entail colleagues standing up at the meetings and telling the faculty about the good works of a fellow colleague. It may take ten minutes of the faculty meeting, but these ten minutes of shout-outs create a culture of celebration and appreciation, thus helping to build the foundation for the cultural change you desire. And as the school leader, don't forget to show up to those meetings on a regular basis as much as possible. Your presence provides gravitas to the agenda and lets people know that you care.

Moreover, inject into those meetings language that promotes the cherished values of the school and embraces the story that constituents can enthusiastically support. If a new idea is proposed, be sure to ask questions, such as "Does this new idea fit into the mission of our school?" "Does the new direction comport with our values?" or "Who should we embrace to vet the new idea to ensure that people will want to opt in?"

I highly recommend the many works of Lee Bolman and Terrence Deal on reframing organizations and Robert Richman's book *The Culture Blueprint*. From Bolman and Deal we learn about the frames of change, including political, structural, human resources, and symbolic. I have found reliance on these frames to be essential for successful change management. From Richman we learn that culture happens within the context of the community of any institution. He uses the example of Zappos, the largest shoe seller in the world. He describes how every worker, no matter their portfolio or position, creates culture. So, too, in our schools, culture is, in essence, the people who reside within it.

Culture change may take a year or seven years. Don't be discouraged. I believe if you customize the ideas, language, and values described within the pages of this book to fit your needs, they can provide the *principles* for the beginning of cultural change or a pathway for enhancement of your school current culture, story, and values.

Questions for Crafting Your Culture

1. How does your school own its culture and values?
2. What can be added to the *hows* of manifesting your culture?
3. Who is in charge—person or team—of how culture is disseminated throughout your school?
4. How might a guest immediately grasp how culture is done at your school?
5. How are you involving all constituents in *how* your school's culture is created and sustained?
6. How can you do better at this? What steps might you take to shape your school culture?

5

Parents and Grandparents
Partners in Raising A+ Human Beings

Parents

Over my eighteen years as founding head of de Toledo High School, my admissions department would set up speaking engagements for me, usually on the theme of raising moral teenagers. These talks had three purposes: to emphasize the crucial partnership between home and school in our goal of raising A+ human beings; to provide a free service to the community; and to serve as a "soft" student recruitment vehicle for the school. I usually gave five talks each year in various parts of Los Angeles.

In preparation for these talks, I sat down with our youngest daughter, Rebecca, then in ninth grade, and asked for her guidance. She was the fourth child, fourteen years younger than her oldest sibling, so I figured that perhaps by then my wife and I had figured out how to do some things right in parenting. Since Rebecca was the beneficiary of all that wisdom and experience, perhaps she might have some ideas on what to include in my talks.

Over a dinner of sushi, spring rolls, and tea, Rebecca created on a napkin the outline for raising moral children using the acronym PAVES:

Parent
Actions
Values
Expectations
Supper

At the beginning of each of my talks, which usually took place at local synagogues, I would write PAVES on a large whiteboard and proceed to explain.

Parent: Continuity and Being Proactive Matter

My experience teaches me that most of children's behaviors are a direct result of parental guidance and actions. Yes, peer pressure certainly has an impact, but what parents say and do makes a much greater difference.

For many parents attending my talks, this came as quite a surprise. Some of the parents believed that once their kids become teens, they no longer had any control. They reasoned that peer pressure would overtake whatever values they had taught their children since birth. I wanted them to know that their encouragement at home would reinforce the values we teach in the school and that they undoubtedly supported: to be kind, to avoid gossip, to reject cliques, and to strive to become A+ human beings.

For some, this revelation was a great relief and a motivation to continue to parent proactively. For others, it was a source of fear that they were, indeed, still in charge and that they could not stop proactively parenting during the high school years.

I then explained further that years ago, brain researchers found that the human brain did not become fully formed in the area of judgment until age twenty-five. (I always added that it most likely took men until age forty; this always received a good chuckle, especially from the women in the room.) Wasn't it odd that even though this fact was well documented, it did not prevent states from allowing kids to drive at age sixteen, vote at age eighteen, and drink at age twenty-one? Yet in California you must be twenty-five to rent a car. I suppose that only the car rental companies took the research seriously.

Of course, the point of this opening to my talk was simple and clear: Continue to be a parent. Continue to impart limitations, rules, and wisdom. And understand that in the long run, your kids will thank you for standing strong.

I closed this part of the talk with a powerful real-life story I heard from a recovering alcoholic. Joe (not his real name) explained to me that his father had always told him never to drink alcohol and drive. His father also told him that at any time of day or night, he would pick him up if he were drunk and unable to safely operate his car. Sure enough, Joe never drove drunk. He never received a DUI. Yet, Joe explained, he still became an alcoholic. It seems his father never told Joe not to drink. Without saying so, Joe's father provided tacit approval for him to abuse alcohol. Joe's dad believed that since "all" teens drink, so too would Joe, so why tell him not to? His father only wanted to ensure that Joe made it home safely.

When Joe tells his story to high school kids and their parents, he closes in a rueful tone: "I wish my dad would have told me not to drink, and why. By assuming I would drink, my dad had given me permission, and in my not-fully-mature teenage brain, that permission made all the difference."

Actions: Promoting Your School Culture's Values at Home

Children are like "God"—they see everything parents do. Kids miss nothing and mimic every parental action: If a parent curses, then kids will curse. If parents smoke, then it's okay to smoke. If parents drive too fast, then it's okay to drive too fast. The following is also true: If parents give to charity, kids will give. If parents speak with kindness, so will their kids. If parents avoid gossip, so too will their kids. If parents provide unconditional love, their children will love them and others unconditionally.

In my talks to parents, I often offered two personal examples: one painful, the other joyful.

Several years ago, while driving with one of my daughters, I asked her why she always drove five miles per hour over the speed limit. She turned to me with a puzzled look and an impish smile and said, "Dad, I drive too fast because you do." Ouch!! Today that daughter is a responsible adult with children of her own. Thank God, she finally rejected my actions and today she drives more carefully than I ever did.

On a more positive note, another one of our daughters came home from her elementary school one day and as usual we asked her about her day. She described how one of her friends was being shunned by the "in" group on the schoolyard. Our daughter was very upset about this and marched up to the "in" crowd of girls and scolded them for being mean to her friend. My wife and I were amazed by her courage and resilience. "What happened after that?" we asked. "Oh," she replied, "I got everyone together and made peace. Now we are all friends again." "What made you do this?" we asked. She responded, "Because I always see how Mom speaks to the women in the PTA, being kind and making peace. So I figured I could do the same thing."

Today that daughter is a professional mediator.

Values Are Taught and Caught

In my talks, after driving home the point about the importance of parental actions, I moved on to values. I explained that what we ask our kids when they come home from school each day is a tacit indication to our children of what we value. If we ask, "How was math class today?" then we value math. If we ask, "Did you make any new friends today," then we value friendship.

I encouraged families to sit down with their children and talk about what their families valued: "What is important to us? What would make us all proud, and what would bring us shame?" I urged them to fully engage their children in this conversation, making appropriate allowances depending on the ages of their kids.

I then suggested that parents ask the following question when their kids come home from school: "Did you do a mitzvah [good deed] today?" Such a question sends a powerful message to their children about what their family truly values. Yes, math is important, as are all the academic subjects and extracurricular activities. However, over a lifetime, what will give life meaning and purpose? What will continue to motivate us? What will promote a world of kindness and strong community?

By prompting such a discussion—rarely done in our work-a-day worlds of carpools, after-school activities, dinner making, and wage earning—the entire family is provided time to reflect, to consider their behaviors in the world, and most importantly, to clarify those values our family expects us all to live by.

Beyond discussion, there is action. Students are keen observers of adults, both at school and at home. They notice if we are walking our talk. Just as the teachers and staff of the school must model the values of the caring culture we work to create, so too kids will "catch" the values parents instill in a family culture of kindness, excellence, and mitzvah.

The Giving Son—Bruce

I had given advice to parents for many years, especially my suggestion that everyone ask their children, "Did you do a mitzvah today?" Of course, like the shoemaker's children who go without shoes, I had never asked my own children this question. It was time I changed that."

Our son was a senior in high school when I tried the question on him. At this point he had been in a Jewish day school since age three, and I was hoping that almost fifteen years of Jewish education would have somehow made its mark.

So I asked him, "Jonny, did you do a mitzvah today?"

He responded with this story: It was the time of year when the seniors were planning their prom. Some of the boys were tasked with finding safe transportation to the prom and ensuring that everyone was included in a limo or party bus. They also were in charge of collecting the forty dollars per person for the limo. Our son found out through a friend that one of the boys could not afford the forty dollars and was planning on having his parents drop him off at the prom instead of joining the gang in a limo.

"What did you do about this?" I asked.

He explained that he quietly, without anyone knowing, gave an additional forty dollars to the boy collecting the money for the limo and told the friend who could not afford the limo that they had collected enough to cover everyone.

Then Jonny asked us, "Does this count as a mitzvah?"

Expectations: Be Clear on What and Why

Perhaps the most difficult part of parenting, especially parenting teens, is to set clear expectations. Of course, the challenge is to ensure those expectations comport with the values of our family, are achievable by our children, and become baked into the DNA of our parenting vision.

Such expectations can fall on a spectrum of simple to complex. For example, we might expect younger children to help set the table, fold the napkins, and clear their own plates from the table after meals. For preteens, we might expect them to take out the trash, do their homework, spend less than an hour a day on social media (good luck with that), and so forth. And for older teens, we might set a curfew, set expectations for good grades, and make rules about use of an automobile.

But does *every* expectation we set align with the values held by our family? For example, if we believe in the importance of community as a value, then clearing the table and taking out the trash align with contributing to the family community. In other words, let's be sure to place whatever expectations we make into the context of our family's values *and* be sure to explain to our kids how we arrived at those expectations.

Perhaps among the most complex expectations are those parents set on their teens regarding getting good grades. Is the expectation for all As, or is the expectation to "work hard and do your best"?

I once saw a fabulous cartoon in a magazine. It was a drawing of five animals—an elephant, a monkey, a cat, a bird, and a horse—standing in front of a tree. The caption read, "I expect everyone to climb this tree." The message was humorous but clear—the elephant could not climb the tree but he could certainly knock it over; the monkey was up the tree in a flash; the cat found its way up but couldn't get down; the bird didn't climb but simply could fly to the top; and the horse could not climb the tree but was happy to offer a ride home to everyone else—except, of course, the elephant.

At school, we set concrete expectations of student behavior and achievement. When parents set expectations based on our family's values, and more importantly on the unique gifts of each of our children, we establish powerful guideposts as we navigate the parenting journey.

Supper: Quality and Quantity Time Makes the Difference

Finally, in my presentations I talked about "supper," which is really a metaphor for quality and quantity time with our kids.

Several years back, a researcher discovered an interesting trend regarding the characteristics of those students who are selected as National Merit scholarship winners. (This award is based on students' PSAT and SAT scores along with grades and some letters of recommendation. Each winner receives money toward college tuition and gains prestige by being one of only eight thousand kids in the nation to receive the award each year.) We can all assume that these students are academically gifted, hard workers, good test takers, and overall good kids. What the researchers did not expect to find was that the majority of these children had dinner together with their families on a regular basis. In other words, time with parents and siblings made a difference.

Whereas all families have widely varying lives and time commitments, it is clear that spending regular time with our children is vital for their intellectual and emotional development. I often call this "tuck-in time." Most of us remember tucking in our younger children at bedtime. We would sit on the side of the bed, read a story, talk about their day, or simply share some news about friends or feelings about what happened that day. Dinner together with our kids, quiet moments before bedtime, walks together around the block, or any other time a family can carve out is a form of tuck-in time. And most kids, even teenagers, love it. They appreciate the special attention and unconditional, nonjudgmental caring from their parents.

For many families where both parents work, or there is a single parent or guardian, or the parents are divorced—to mention only a few family structures—time with our children can be challenging but should still remain an important priority. This time provides the emotional anchor children require and also offers opportunity for parents to transmit, in subtle and overt ways, important values that children can use when facing the many challenges they will encounter in their lives.

The Adult Children Who Still Want Tuck-In Time—Bruce

I was having a conversation with some friends of ours, and they told me that they had made tuck-in time almost a religion in their home. They had four children, now all adults with children of their own. Our friends described a time when their son, a highly accomplished professional, brought his family over to their house for Shabbat and planned to sleep over with his wife and two kids. On Friday night, once his own kids were in bed and our friends had also adjourned to their own beds, in walked their grown son, who sat down on the end of his parents' bed. They asked him, "What are you doing here?" He replied, "I'd just like to talk and catch up. A lot has been going on at work and I'd like to process it with you." In other words, their son wanted tuck-in time, even as an adult. Our friends continued to tell us that all four of their kids, all of whom are married with children of their own, call their mother, and sometimes their father, almost every day just to check in.

Indeed, the power of "supper" together and the memories and importance of tuck-in time continued to resonate and provide an anchor for a lifetime.

A Final Word on Parenting

As we all know, parenting is hard work. Children do not come with a user manual, and we can all attest to the fact that sometimes children are not always "user friendly." As we all reflect on how best to raise our kids,

I hope that PAVES (Parent, Actions, Values, Expectations, Supper) will be an easy memory aid to help pave the way to success.

Perhaps the most important action I did not include in the PAVES approach is parents' unconditional love for our children and being sure we continuously communicate that love in a variety of ways. When a teen yells "I hate you" at you because everyone else gets to stay out until 1 a.m. and you have set the curfew for midnight, a good response might be "I love you too. At least you know how much we care about you."

Moreover, a parent's love is not only unconditional but also non-judgmental. Parents never compare their children with anyone else. There are, of course, expectations, but just like the story of the five animals and the tree, parents recognize the unique gifts in each of their children and create expectations based on those gifts. No matter what, parents' love can never be conditioned on achieving or not achieving the expectations; the love is unconditional.

Now imagine parents who lovingly supervise and guide their children at every turn, who themselves set the highest examples of moral and ethical behavior, who share and engage their children in discussions of good values, who are clear in their expectations, and who carve out significant time to spend with their kids. When such parents do this, they are indispensable partners with the school in raising A+ human beings. I believe that such parents will change the world, and with some luck thrown in, their children will honor their parents for eternity.

Grandparents: Supporting School Culture with Love and Wisdom

Ellen Howard, the long-serving principal at de Toledo High School, is in charge of the annual "Generations Day." This is a moment to show off the school, but more importantly to embrace grandparents, special friends, and perhaps aunts and uncles into the school culture and vision. Ellen opens the program, in part, with the following words:

For students to be leaders, they must be willing to take risks. For them to feel comfortable taking risks, they must have self-esteem. As you are here today for them, it is your generation that helps them build their self-esteem. You do not need to worry about such parental pleasures as a messy room, sloppy homework, or staying out after curfew. Who but your generation accepts them unconditionally and thinks everything they do is perfect? You play an important role in dispensing wisdom.

Indeed, this is one of my favorite programs of the year. Cool high school students, who tend to ignore their parents if they come on campus, turn to mush around your generation. No problem giving you hugs and kisses or holding your hand in public.

Even though not all of you here are grandparents, I think this quote applies to all. A former New York mayor said, "What children need most are the essentials that grandparents provide in abundance. They give unconditional love, kindness, patience, humor, comfort, lessons in life. And most importantly, cookies."

In many ways, it is the unconditional love and patience, life lessons, and humor that punctuate a school's culture. It is a moment for the students to observe how their school honors those of another generation, how their school shows appreciation, and how their school values legacy, the continuity of history, and the essential bonds of family and community. In many ways, so much of the school's culture is practiced and symbolized by this special day.

The Secret—Ron

Our grandchildren, Ellie and Gabe Hall, attend the Gideon Hausner Jewish Day School in Palo Alto, California. My wife, Susie, and I have always looked forward to Grandparents and Special Friends Day. We are invited to visit the classrooms, tour the campus, even enjoy a Torah study class taught by one of the Jewish studies teachers. The highlight of the day is an all-school assembly featuring performances by the different grade levels—an exciting way to show off the talents of the kids—and a short testimonial about the school from a grateful veteran grandparent. One year, David Zimand, the head of school at the time, invited me to speak in this slot and I eagerly accepted. As Susie and I entered the gym for the assembly with Ellie and our daughter, Havi, the room was filling rapidly with the several hundred children, hundreds of grandparents and parents, and the entire staff of the school. When it came time for my talk, David began to introduce me by reading my usual bio, but then he suddenly stopped, looked up from his notes, and said, "I need a little help to properly introduce Dr. Wolfson. Ellie Hall, would you please join me?" In a flash, Ellie jumped out of her front-row seat, ran up to the podium in front of six hundred people, grabbed the microphone, and in her sweet voice said, "Well, he is my grandfather, but I call him Zaydie." And then, like the announcer on the TV show *The Price Is Right* yelling "Come on down!" Ellie raised her voice and concluded, "He's Rahhhhhhhn Wolfson!"

The place exploded with applause and cheers—not for me but for Ellie's heartfelt, sweet, and assured poise in the moment. I looked at Mommy Havi as if to ask, "Did you know about this?" No, it was a secret between the head of school and Ellie! I ran up to Ellie, gave her a huge hug and kiss on the *keppie*, and declared to the audience, "That was the best introduction I've had in fifty years of public speaking! Thank you, Ellie!" I then spent my five minutes raving about how our grandchildren were flourishing under the guidance of the terrific teachers and encouraged my fellow grandparents to join me in what I like to call "Bring Your Checkbook to School Day" by donating to the institution in honor of our grandkids. It was a memorable moment, funds were raised, and I was so proud of Ellie!

Ask—They Want to Help

Schools often hesitate to use Grandparents Day to engender support. Some believe it is simply a time for the grandparents to *kvell*, not for grandparents to be bothered with the exigencies surrounding a school's need for constant financial support.

I have a different view. As a grandparent, I am disappointed if the school does not invite us to join some kind of "giving circle." In so many cases, parents struggle to pay tuition and fees and to fund all of the extracurricular activities offered to today's children. Grandparents are usually at a stage of life where those expenses are no longer a daily burden. Many have developed a modicum of wealth, and almost all want to support the education of their grandkids. Why wouldn't they? Believe me, no one should feel embarrassed about asking. If done in a dignified manner, everyone goes away feeling good. And asking people to give is an essential part of the school's culture and values.

A Unique Complement to Education

On another practical note, grandparents can play powerful supporting roles in building an all-encompassing educational environment. In this day and age of technology, no matter where one lives, grandparents can communicate with their grandchildren on a regular basis.

Imagine the excitement and opportunity for learning for the grandchild who is passionate about space travel and then learns from her grandfather that he actually witnessed the first moon launch on a black-and-white TV set way back in 1969.

Or imagine how much can be taught by grandparents who download "Social Chess" on their smartphones and teach their grandkids how to play the game, how to strategize, and most importantly, how to think broadly about the world. I can only imagine the rich discussions that might emanate from such communications.

For those grandkids excited about sports, what fun it would be to hear from their grandparents that they were actually at the football stadium watching fifth-ranked UCLA led by Gary Beban upset undefeated Michigan State in the Rose Bowl in 1966 and making that a jumping off point to trace more recent moments in college football history.

The possibilities to enhance our grandchildren's education are endless. Whether talking about our professional, business, artistic, military, or any aspect of our past working lives can add so much depth to children's education—and grandparents typically have the time and patience to impart their knowledge and skills.

Of course, most importantly, grandparents are there to impart wisdom. The development of wisdom is certainly part of the culture of any great school, so who better to enhance that culture than those who have lived lives of intentionality, made mistakes, met hundreds of our fellow human beings throughout their lives, and have gained experience and wisdom in how to navigate life's pathways.

Family History—Bruce

The COVID-19 crisis of 2020 meant that many children spent most of their days at home, taking classes online. Debby and I saw this as an opportunity to spend quality time with some of the older grandkids, ages eight through fourteen, giving them an overview of our family's history and legacy. We learned how to set up a Powerpoint slideshow, share it on Zoom, and set times to "meet" with four of the kids to share with them the history of their great-grandparents and of us. We found photos of old neighborhoods, old cars, TV sets, houses where their great-grandparents lived and grew up (the wonders of Google Earth), and we engaged the kids in conversations about life then and now. We also talked about the political and social history of the times, World War II (both great-grandfathers served on Guadalcanal, in the Solomon Islands, in 1942), and how one of their great-grandmothers created the gift store at a major hospital in Los Angeles and the other raised millions of dollars for ORT, an organization that runs eight hundred vocational schools.

These sessions not only generated family pride and connection but also allowed us to explain the culture of our families and how that culture is also woven into the fabric of their lives, families, and schools.

Questions for Crafting Your Culture

1. How would you articulate the culture of your family?
2. What are the core values and components of your family culture?
3. What are the signature features of your family culture?
4. What would you like to add to your family culture?
5. What do your children and grandchildren know of their legacy?
6. What do they know of their family history?
7. What evidence do you have that they know the values their parents and grandparents cherish?
8. What steps can be taken to empower our families to share family legacy, history, and values with our children?
9. How can the school ensure meaning and purpose in the lives of our children?

AFTERWORD

All of us reside in a multiplicity of cultural contexts. We are products of our families, cities, states, nations, religious backgrounds, languages, politics, genders, race, and ultimately our world. My guess is that once humans inhabit the moon or Mars, or planets beyond, we will add yet another dimension to our particularistic and pluralistic cultures.

Our schools and institutions are microcosms of unique culture usually residing within the contexts of the local community and city. Although the school is a relatively small part of the overall culture in which we live, it may be, next to family, the most powerful and effective shaper of a child's world. If we assume that is the case, then the importance of a school's culture becomes magnified far beyond its seemingly small stature and resonance. And, by extension, the work of the professionals, parents, teachers, and board who shape the school become influencers in how we raise our children.

We hope this book has provided guideposts, pathways, ideas, and visions for *what* makes a positive, values-driven school culture, *who* constitutes the culture makers within and outside the school, what language might be useful, and *how* it might all combine to establish an educational context that is far richer, deeper, and more effective than our traditional concept of what constitutes educational greatness.

Clearly we believe that the ultimate educational outcome of a culture of academic excellence and AP kindness is to shape A+ human beings. This view is not to diminish the wisdom of the philosopher Josiah Royce, a quote carved above the entrance to Royce Hall at UCLA: "Education is learning to use those tools which the civilization has found indispensable." Academic knowledge and skills, artistic expressions, strong bodies, and the ability to analyze, synthesize, and evaluate continue to be pillars of our educational processes. However, we believe that these pillars within a cultural vacuum develop students without an understanding of what it's all for—the meaning and purpose of math or science, for example—unless they exist within a cultural milieu that provides meaning, direction, and wisdom for using those indispensable tools. We believe that what makes them indispensable is the culture, the values, and ultimate applications of those tools found in the wisdom of culture.

In our view, the work of education is a sacred task. If done within the context of a positive and meaningful culture, its sacred nature becomes apparent to our students. If done without the guidance of culture, if done in a vacuum bereft of wisdom and purpose, we create students who are vacuous—they possess tools but no motivation to use them for the good; they possess skills that, if used without the wisdom found within a positive and meaningful culture, can lead them onto dangerous paths.

On the other hand, students who are embraced within a wise and meaningful culture—who learn the language, values, and practices we have described here—will be equipped to describe for themselves and others the purpose of their work and by extension their lives. They emerge with initiative and motivation to use their knowledge, skills, and kindness to improve a broken world. They emerge as contributors to the greater culture of the Jewish people and the nations we live in. They become builders and shapers of both Jewish and secular values; thoughtful and vital participants in the great conversations within our democratic process. Indeed, students raised within an embracing school culture graduate as leaders of the future.

Finally, students educated within a vibrant school culture become souls on fire—souls that leave a legacy of good, souls that care, and souls that ultimately embody all that we seek to imbue within them, to our most precious next generation, our legacy.

ACKNOWLEDGMENTS

We gratefully acknowledge the expertise and encouragement of those who helped us craft this book. Stuart Matlins, founder of Jewish Lights Publishing, is an extraordinary consultant whose wise counsel improved every aspect of this project. He recruited the talented book editor Emily Wichland, whose attention to detail elevated our content and language, and Tim Holtz, who designed a beautiful book and cover. Dan Medwin supervised the marketing.

We thank the colleagues and friends who read early drafts of the manuscript and who favored us with contributions and endorsements: Dr. Erica Rothblum, Betty Winn, Mark Shpall, Tammy Shpall, Harlene Appelman, Cheryl Finkel, Dr. Gil Graff, Rabbi Edward Feinstein, Paul Bernstein, Jeff Lefkowitz, Gregg Alpert, Michael Brooks, Donniel Hartman, Havi Hall, Ellen Howard, David Bryfman, Dr. Josh Elkin, and Dr. Rachel Lerner.

Bruce Powell

A special thank you to the founding board, faculty, and families who crafted the original culture of excellence and kindness at de Toledo High School/New Community Jewish High School. The founding board members and major founding donors include Howard and Rebekah Farber, Harold and Amy Masor Mike Greenfeld, Judy Greenfeld, Elana Rimmon Zimmerman, Scott Zimmerman, Jeffrey and Allyn Levine, Faith and Jon

Cookler, Earl Greinetz (z"l), Dave Aberson, David Marcus, Eddy Klein, Pam and Mark Teitelbaum, Shirley Levine (z"l), Marty Lasker, Bernard Gero, Gary Polson, Sheila Kurland, David Krygier, and the Jewish Federation of Greater Los Angeles under the leadership of John Fishel and Jay Sanderson. And enormous gratitude to Jake (z"l) and Janet Farber and Ellie and Mark Lainer, true community visionaries.

The founding faculty and staff members include Dr. Bill Aron, Hyim Brandes, Kathi Edwards, Benny Ferdman, Dr. Neil Kramer, Michelle Lindner, Gabe Lynn, Sina Monjazeb, Mark Shpall, Eric Sloate, Rabbi David Vorspan, Jill Zuckerman, Lisa Ansell, David Dassa, Dr. Michael Isaacson, Suzy Bookbinder, Evi Klein, Brian McGraw, Dvorah Okun, Emily Powell, Terrylene Sacchetti, Dana Wexler, and Suzy Bookbinder.

A special thank you to my educational mentor, Dr. Shlomo Bardin (z"l), founder of the Brandeis-Bardin Institute of the American Jewish University, a visionary educator from whom I learned how to create a vision and who created a place where, for the past sixty years, Debby and I found each other at Brandeis-Bardin, raised our kids, and brought Shlomo's teachings into our home.

Thank you to my parents, Jim and Bea Powell (z"l), and Debby's parents, Dr. Ludwig and Ada Strauss (z"l), who set the foundations for our lives in word and deed.

And, of course, I want to acknowledge the generosity and vision of the de Toledo Family, Alyce, Phil, Aaron, and Ben, which has ensured the legacy of de Toledo High School for years to come.

Ron Wolfson

I wish to thank the people in my life who taught me the importance of crafting culture, beginning with my beloved parents, Bernice and Alan Wolfson, who taught me and my brothers, Bob and Doug, a lifelong course in AP kindness—our memories of them will forever be a blessing. Rabbi Bernard Lipnick (z"l), the powerhouse leader of Congregation B'nai Amoona in St. Louis, trusted me to shape a unique culture for teenagers and changed my life. Dr. Louis M. Smith, my esteemed professor of education at Washington University in St. Louis, guided my deep dive into the literature of enculturation. My thanks to Rabbi Ron Stern of Stephen Wise Temple for introducing us to Will Pernell, a spectacular creator of welcoming culture, in a video I have shared with hundreds of Jewish leaders throughout the world. And, of course, I am grateful for the many students and colleagues I have been privileged to learn with over forty-five years at American Jewish University.

Ron and Bruce

We are both blessed to be on faculty of the American Jewish University in Los Angeles, whose president, Dr. Jeffrey Herbst, and the dean of the Graduate Center for Jewish Education, Dr. Rachel Lerner, encourage collaborative scholarship. We thank them and our colleagues on the AJU faculty and board.

The Kripke Institute, devoted to Jewish literacy and Jewish education, is a tribute to the legacy of Rabbi Myer S. Kripke and Dorothy K. Kripke (z"l), who believed in the power of words to shape the character of children and families. Special thanks to our dear friends Ellie and Mark Lainer, giants among the supporters of Jewish education, who generously supported the publication and distribution of this book.

Our deepest thanks to Rabbi Elaine Zecher, senior rabbi of Temple Israel in Boston, for her inspiring teaching in the foreword.

We are grateful to Valley Beth Shalom's Rabbi Ed Feinstein—the founding head of school of the Ann and Nate Levine Academy who was so beloved in Dallas, the street in front of this outstanding day school is named in his honor—for his insightful and inspiring words in the preface. Ann and Nate—thanks for everything!

Writing a book requires hours upon hours of time away from our families. We thank them for their forbearance, their support, and their love: Debby Powell; Rachel and Avi Gereboff and their children, Yonah, Rami, and Elan; Naomi and Seth Strongin, and their children Lilah, Nathan, and Harrison; Jonathan and Michal Berkson Powell and their children, Ezra and Isaac; Rebecca Powell and Aloni Cohen; Susie Wolfson;

Michael Wolfson and Regina Pruss; and Havi Wolfson Hall, David Hall, Ellie Hall, and Gabe Hall.

Finally, we thank you for all you do to raise A+ human beings by crafting cultures of excellence and kindness in your communities!

APPENDIX A

THE CULTURE AUDIT

As stated throughout the book, schools do not give grades for how students do in comporting with the culture of the place. That said, maybe we should. Or we might at least consider doing our own internal "culture audit." Below are some categories to be shared with your staff to help determine how your school is doing. We are sure there are many more categories to add depending on your unique circumstances.

Grade your school on the following:

- Personal welcoming from any and all staff upon arrival
- Personal welcoming from students
- First official contact with office receptionist
- Directional signage
- Symbols, art, and colors throughout the building
- Overall decor and cleanliness (at least before lunch)
- Donor walls and other honorary plaques
- Open office doors
- Continuous "culture education" for all personnel
- Physical location of offices
- Sense of embrace
- Culture of kindness among faculty and students
- Lunchtime culture of kindness: Does anyone sit alone?
- Circles of friends versus cliques

- Use of language: Do faculty and students "own" the cultural language of the school?
- Swag
- Ritual activities including graduation, open houses, and services
- Food service
- Student store
- Volunteers on campus

This list could go on and on, but you get the idea. Have fun with this and add those cultural touch points vital to your school.

APPENDIX B

THE A+ HUMAN BEING REPORT CARD

Schools do not usually grade their students on what kind of human beings they are. But what would happen if we did? What would such a report card look like? What would be the key criteria for such a grade?

Below is a suggested set of criteria for such a report card. Please develop your own based on your school's values and culture. Keep in mind that our use of a "report card" is only a metaphor to determine how we are doing in what we believe to be a core function of schools—that is, building A+ human beings.

Grade your students on the following:

- Kindness
- Openness to new friendships; expanding one's circle of friends
- Volunteering mentality
- Initiative in leadership
- Collaboration and cooperation
- Respect for teachers, staff, janitors, security personnel, each other
- Integrity
- Eagerness to learn; desire to teach others
- Courage in the face of unkindness or someone bullying another
- "Bucket filler" or "bucket dipper"—one who gives or one who takes
- "Thermometer" or "Thermostat"—one who reflects the "temperature" or one who sets the "temperature"

- Seeing each fellow student or worker as created in the "image of God"
- Honesty in all aspects of "school business"
- Performing regular acts of loving-kindness
- Care in use of language
- Understanding of one's obligations to the community, not just one's rights
- Seeking meaning
- Seeking of wisdom

NOTES

Introduction

1. The story of the Vov class is told in Bernard Lipnick, *An Experiment in Teenage Religious Education* (New York: Block Publishing, 1976).

Chapter 2: The *What* of Values

1. Chesley Sullenberger III, "Saving Flight 1549," interview by Katie Couric, *60 Minutes*, CBS, February 8, 2009.

2. Joseph Telushkin, *Words That Hurt, Words That Heal: How the Words You Choose Shape Your Destiny* (New York: William Morrow, 2019).

3. Joseph Fletcher, *Situation Ethics: The New Morality* (Louisville, KY: Westminster John Knox Press, 1997).

4. Abraham Joshua Heschel, *The Sabbath* (New York: Farrar, Straus and Giroux, 2005).

Chapter 3: The *Who*: Creators of Embracing School Culture

1. John Nemo, "What a NASA Janitor Can Teach Us about Living a Bigger Life," *The Business Journals*, December 23, 2014, https://www.bizjournals.com/bizjournals/how-to/growth-strategies/2014/12/what-a-nasa-janitor-can-teach-us.html.

Chapter 4: The *How* of Building and Sustaining School Culture

1. "Where Everybody Knows Your Name," written by Gary Portnoy and Judy Hart Angelo, performed by Gary Portnoy, *Cheers*, 1983.

2. See Ronald G. Wolfson, "An Innovative Living Experience in Israel," *Journal of Jewish Education*, January 2007.

SELECTED BIBLIOGRAPHY

Bolman, Lee, and Terrence Deal. *How Great Leaders Think: The Art of Reframing.* San Francisco: Jossey-Bass, 2014.

Collins, Jim. *Good to Great.* New York: Harper Business, 2001.

Deal, Terrence, and Kent D. Peterson. *Shaping School Culture.* San Francisco: Jossey-Bass, 1999.

Gladwell, Malcolm, *David and Goliath: Underdogs, Misfits, and the Art of Battling Giants.* Boston: Little Brown, 2013.

Lipnick, Bernard. *An Experiment in Teenage Religious Education.* New York: Block Publishing, 1976.

Parker, Priya. *The Art of Gathering: How We Meet and Why It Matters.* New York: Riverhead Books, 2018.

Richman, Robert. *The Culture Blueprint, Version 1.5: A Guide to Building the High-Performance Workplace.* Minneapolis, MN: Culture Hackers, 2015.

Saphier, Jon, and Matthew King. "Good Seeds Grow in Strong Cultures." *Educational Leadership* 42, no. 6 (March 1985): 67–74.

Wolfson, Ron. *Relational Judaism: Using the Power of Relationships to Transform the Jewish Community.* Woodstock, VT: Jewish Lights, 2013.

Wolfson, Ron. *The Spirituality of Welcoming: How to Transform Your Congregation into a Sacred Community.* Woodstock, VT: Jewish Lights, 2007.

Wolfson, Ronald G. "A Description and Analysis of an Innovative Living Experience in Israel: The Dream and the Reality." PhD dissertation, Washington University, 1974. University Microfilms, 1980.

Pirkei Avot, any edition

Notes

Notes

Notes

A WORD ABOUT
THE KRIPKE INSTITUTE

One day in 1953, Susie Buffett, the wife of the famous Warren Buffett, walked into a bookstore and discovered a thin volume titled *Let's Talk about God* by Dorothy K. Kripke, the wife of Rabbi Myer S. Kripke, the rabbi of Beth El Synagogue in Omaha, Nebraska. She brought it home and read it to her daughter Susie, who loved the book. Noticing that the author was local, Mrs. Buffett called Mrs. Kripke to invite her for a cup of coffee. (Today we would call their meeting a "one-to-one.") The two women immediately hit it off and hatched a plan to get together again, this time with their husbands. They explored their interests and passions to see if there was one they shared. Their common ground: bridge. And so the Kripkes and the Buffetts—who, it turns out, lived within a few blocks of each other—began to play bridge together on a regular basis. Over those bridge games, they became close friends, even sharing annual Thanksgiving dinners together at the Buffetts, Susie making tuna fish casseroles in lieu of turkey for the kashrut-observant rabbi and his wife.

When Warren established his investment groups, Dorothy encouraged the rabbi to invest a modest inheritance with his friend. The rabbi resisted, not wishing to mix business with friendship. Warren, too, would say that he was leery of having his friends in the investment group . . . in case things went bad. They didn't go bad. Finally the rabbi asked Warren to invest his savings, converting his stake into shares of Berkshire Hathaway, Buffett's holding company. The small investment turned into millions of unexpected dollars, which the Kripkes began generously giving away in 1997.

On one of my visits to Omaha, I suggested to Rabbi Kripke that he consider funding an institute to honor Dorothy's extraordinary contributions to Jewish children's and family literature. He readily agreed and we created the Dorothy K. and Myer S. Kripke Institute for Jewish Family Literacy, which I have the honor to lead. We established a National Jewish Book Award in Dorothy's memory. We fund the Omaha branch of the outstanding PJ Library program of building Jewish family libraries. Most recently, the Center for Relational Judaism was founded to support the research that resulted in the publication of *Relational Judaism* and *The Relational Judaism Handbook,* and to be a resource hub for those doing the important work of relational engagement. With the publication of *Raising A+ Human Beings,* we are creating the Institute for School Culture to support this crucial work in Jewish education. We hope The Kripke Institute is a fitting echo of that first "coffee date" between Susie Buffett and Dorothy Kripke so many years ago.

ABOUT THE AUTHORS

Dr. Bruce Powell

For the past fifty years, Bruce has dedicated his professional life to Jewish education in settings from day schools to synagogue schools to summer camps.

He has helped to found and lead three Jewish high schools and has consulted on the founding of twenty-three more throughout North America. In addition, he has provided consulting services to over sixty Jewish day schools through his work as president of Jewish School Management (JSM).

Honored with both the Covenant Foundation Award and the Milken Jewish Educator Award, Bruce has served as a founding faculty member and mentor for the Day School Leadership Training Institute at The Jewish Theological Seminary, and as a coach for the Head of School Professional Excellence Project at Prizmah. He directs the Institute for Day School Excellence and Sustainability (IDEAS) and serves as Distinguished Lecturer of Jewish Education at the American Jewish University.

Together with his wife, Debby, they share four children and have invested an aggregate of fifty-two child-years in Jewish day school education for their kids. Their grandchildren now attend Jewish day schools in Los Angeles.

Dr. Ron Wolfson

Ron is the Fingerhut Professor of Education at American Jewish University and president of The Kripke Institute. He is a much sought-after consultant and lecturer on building relational cultures for Jewish day schools as well as synagogues and their schools, community centers, and camps around the world.

He has had a profound effect on the Jewish community through his books *Relational Judaism: Using the Power of Relationships to Transform the Jewish Community* and *The Relational Judaism Handbook* (with Rabbi Nicole Auerbach and Rabbi Lydia Medwin).

In addition to training clergy and educators, Ron is the author of many books bringing the values and rituals of Jewish life to a popular audience, including *God's To-Do List*, *The Seven Questions You're Asked in Heaven*, *The Spirituality of Welcoming*, and *The Art of Jewish Living* series.

Ron lives in Los Angeles with his wife, Susie. They are the parents of two children and the grandparents of two grandchildren, both day school students.

To order additional copies of *Raising A+ Human Beings*

Additional copies of this book may be ordered by mail prepaid by check only directly from The Kripke Institute at:

The Kripke Institute
Institute for School Culture
5110 Densmore Avenue
Encino, CA 91436

or from our distributor prepaid by check or credit card sent to:

LongHill Partners, Inc.
PO Box 237, Woodstock, VT 05091
tel: 802-457-4000 fax: 802-457-4004
email: awilson@longhillpartners.com

If you would like to explore site visits —virtual or in-person—individualized consulting, or other presentations to help craft your school culture, email us at ronwolfson1234@gmail.com or bpowell@jewishschoolmanagement.com.

QUANTITY & PRICE

 # OF COPIES

_____ × $ _____ = $ _____
(see quantity prices right)

Shipping & Handling* $ _____

Total $ _____   **TOTAL ($)**

1–10 copies: $19.99 per copy
11–29 copies: $17.99 per copy
30+ copies: $16.99 per copy

*Shipping & Handling
Within the U.S.:
Add $3.95 for the first book,
$2.00 each additional book.

SHIP TO
(if different from billing address)

Name _____ (please print all information) _____ Phone _____

Street _____

City _____ State _____ Zip _____

Email _____

METHOD OF PAYMENT
(All orders must be prepaid.)

☐ Check enclosed for $ _____ payable to The Kripke Institute
☐ Charge my credit card: ☐ MasterCard ☐ Visa

Card # _____ CID # _____ Exp. Date _____

Signature _____

Credit card name and billing address are: ☐ Same as shipping ☐ Other:

Name _____ (please print all information) _____ Phone _____

Street _____

City _____ State _____ Zip _____

Email _____